Happy Dance

"Fabulous Through the Seasons"

By Denise Rogers & Debbie Sempsrott

Grins & Giggles, Tears & Triumphs, Hope & Healing

For the Seasons of a Woman's Soul

"Happy Dance" – Second Edition Revised, May 2014

Copyright 2013

Edited by Vicki White (Our third cord, prayer partner, and friend.)

Graphics used with permission by Gretchen Jackson, our amazing sketch artist. (We want to express much appreciation to Gretchen!)

ISBN: 978-0-615-81128-4

Readers Beware!

What readers are saying about

"Happy Dance":

- **Lydia feels lighter**—*"This book will lower your blood pressure while waiting in a dentist or doctor's office … so I keep a copy in my purse!"*

- **Husbands TOO!** — *"My husband picked up this book first and said, 'You've got to stop and listen to this?' He read me the entire first chapter. What a delightful, tender book for women and their listening husbands."*

- **MJ's Hooray**—*"This is a great book … encouraging and funny. The combination of both ladies is what makes it. I can't wait for another."*

- **Be Warned!**—*"I laughed until the tears ran down my legs! People stared at me due to the snorting and loss of breath. What a fun, inspiring book."*

- **Laughing Out Loud in CA**—*"This was an inspiring book that had me laughing from start to finish. Easy read. I couldn't put it down and can't wait to read the next books! Beware of reading this in public places!"*

- **Kicking Cancer**—*"It will make you laugh. It will make you cry. It will make you laugh until you cry. These words of truth from women to women will feed your soul and calm your spirit."*

- **Jail Break**—*"The women in prison just love these authors. They can't wait until we bring more books. They are laughing, listening, and learning."*

So, Readers Beware!

This book may lower your blood pressure,

Make you laugh in public places,

And lighten your load of cares ...

(We invite you to also review this book at Amazon.com)

"There is a time for everything, and a season for every activity under heavens … A time to be born and a time to die … a time to weep and a time to laugh … a time to mourn and a time to DANCE!"—Ecclesiastes 3:1 (NIV)

Wishing you strength for the seasons!

Denise DeHaven Rogers &

Debbie Strater Sempsrott

www.ourfaithfloats.com

Table of Contents

Special Thanks: Vicki White

Preface: Happy Dance

Dedication: Leslie Gilbert

Friends through the Seasons: Meet the Authors

Fabulous through the Seasons: Happy Dance

> **Let's Celebrate . . .** Don't You Look Fabulous (Page 1)
>
> **Winter Winds . . .** Bunny Slopes 101 (Page 12)
>
> **Spring Beginnings . . .** The Spanx Attack (Page 23)
>
> **Summer Heat . . .** It's A Climb (Page 32)
>
> **Autumn Changes . . .** Just Nuke Me Now (Page 43)
>
> **Celebrate Life . . .** Dancin' In the Rain (Page 52)

Faithful through the Seasons: Dedication to Leslie Gilbert (Page 62)

Epilogue: The Changing Seasons (Page 64)

A Prayer for the Seasons (Page 70)

Celebrate the Seasons Studies:

> **Winter . . .** A Time to Wait (Page 71)
>
> **Spring . . .** A Time to Plant (Page 72)
>
> **Summer . . .** A Time to Love (Page 73)
>
> **Fall . . .** A Time to Change (Page 74)

The Barefoot Authors . . . More Book Fun (Page 76)

Debbie Sempsrott

It was the springtime of my life; everything was young and alive with new beginnings when I met Vicki. She was a blessing then, and as only God would have it, she is a blessing to me once again. Vicki and I sang together, prayed together, and became best friends. Then we both moved to different states; Vicki got remarried and changed her last name. It was at that point we lost track of each other. I looked for signs of her existence but I didn't know her last name, what city she lived in, or how to find her. Now, twenty years later we reconnected. How we found each other again could only be God's timing and of God's doing. Not only did we pick up our friendship again, but I found out that editing is Vicki's passion.

God, in His perfect timing, reconnected us during the year that Denise and I were writing this book. I am so privileged to write a book that involves two of my forever friends. I consider every minute of this process a gift from God. How amazing to have a God who shows us faithfulness through the seasons by giving us a partner that is the model of all we are describing. One of my favorite memories of Vicki was when she would laugh and dance (with her pregnant belly jiggling), and now she is the editor for "Happy Dance". God just has a way of making us smile, doesn't He?

Thank you, Vicki, for coming alongside us to edit this book. You make everything flow together with seamless ease. Your editing is much like your friendship; everything is better when your prayerful, loving spirit comes alongside. Our thanks to you, Vicki, is larger than your big ol' home state of Texas.

Preface

Each calendar year is filled with winter, spring, summer, and fall. These seasons spill over into our spiritual, emotional, and physical seasons of life as well. For each and every one of us there is a time to plant, to weep, to laugh, to mourn, and to get up and dance again. Not one of us is going to live on planet earth forever and that awareness brings us fear; fear that comes to steal our faith and rob us of our joy. There is only one match for fear … faith. We need to know that in every season of our lives, *God is still good.*

What is it that we all fear when we face sin, sickness, and suffering? The greatest enemy of life is death. The Bible tells us plainly that the devil cannot take your life, death cannot own your soul, and because the grave could not hold Jesus, it cannot hold you. He defeated the last enemy of sin and death, and that is news worth celebrating.

Perhaps today you find yourself in a place of sadness, sorrow, and suffering. This book is our gift to you because we all need to be reminded that we are never alone. God wants us to know how much He loves us. Many people spend their days in fear worrying about when and how they will die, but the real question for us today is, "What will we do with the seasons of life we have been given?" The devil can't take us and no disease can own us. We belong to God alone. Not one of us is going anywhere until God welcomes us home.

This book is about defeating fear through faith, hope, and love. We hope it brings grins & giggles, tears & triumphs, and hope & healing for the seasons of your soul. This book is filled with laughter and it is all about *"The Dance".*

"A Little Slice of Heaven"

This story is dedicated to our

Dear friend, Leslie Gilbert,

Your love touched our hearts, your joy lifted
us up, and your blog encouraged us all.

This book is for you, sweet girl!

Friends through the Seasons

Meet the Authors:

Denise Rogers & Debbie Sempsrott

Funny Denise . . .

It was wintertime in the desert. The winds were whipping around me, both inside and out. Perhaps you, too, have experienced the winter of your soul? For me, it started in the fall. I had experienced a huge season of change but it was nothing I wanted or had chosen. It came to me quite unexpectedly and it was more than I could begin to deal with.

I was lonely. Our church had lost its minister, my mother and father had moved, and a good friend had relocated far away. My life had taken a turn for the worse with a series of scary decisions that had led me to start my own business. I needed to make it work just to survive. In all of the upheaval, it seemed I had lost my joy and the church was part of the loss. I found it painful now to be at church. People there knew me as the "funny one" and I wasn't feeling humorous, at all.

I needed to get back on the right road … the road that would lead me back to church and help me rediscover my purpose. I had lots of friends, but I really needed a best friend who would help me become what God wanted me to be. I needed the kind of friend that only God could provide. So, I sought God's help, humbly asking for the friend He already knew I needed.

At the same time, Debbie was seeking God's help, but she was praying NOT to come to the desert. I met her in the winter, literally and figuratively. She was the new pastor's wife and she was speaking for our women's brunch. Please understand that I am not putting her down when I say she is not the typical preacher's wife. She can act the part and perform the duties with perfection, but her true character does not align well with that stereotype. As Debbie spoke, I realized she was the friend I had prayed for. Something just clicked. When she told a story about getting caught taking a bubble bath in the baptistery, I howled with laughter. I realized her quirky personality matched mine perfectly, as I am pretty quirky most of the time, too. I never saw her as *the Pastor's wife*. I have always seen her as "Just Debbie".

She is the girl next door who loves to garden, can usually be found swimming in the nearest pool, and is always planning something fun to do. Like me, she is a wife, a mom, and a very busy person who is always involved in a project. She is a singer, a writer, and most of all, my best friend. Debbie is the friend that God sent me in that wintery season of my life. She makes me laugh, and she laughs at my jokes … one more thing I really like about her. We have fun wherever we go. Out of my winter has come a new spring of serving God and writing with my best friend.

We are privileged to write this book together. Debbie is the one who adds the "awe" factor to our stories. She will offer a little glimpse of God's awe-inspiring hand in the everyday things that happen around you, and you will think to yourself, "Awww … I get it." Her writing comes from her gift of encouragement. As for me, I am a born storyteller and comedian at heart. I just love to make people laugh. It's a fun partnership.

Just Debbie . . .

We left beautiful snow and Christmas lights behind us for a house filled with boxes, bone-chilling cold nights, and brown sand blowing in the wind as far as the eye could see. Welcome to winter in the desert. This new, unfamiliar place seemed barren and empty.

No, Toto, we are not in Kansas anymore.

As I went from store to store running errands, the music on the radio was in a different language and the announcements in the stores were not in English. When I walked into the mall for the first time, my cell phone said, "Welcome to Mexico." I was so close to living in a foreign country that my phone could not tell the difference ... neither could I.

It seems almost unbelievable that we can be thoroughly content, enjoying our current season of life and, in the blink of an eye, be transported to another life altogether. Our hearts are ready for Christmas lights and holiday cheer, but instead we only feel the cold winds of winter.

One of the things I find most amazing about God is how He always provides us with special people to bless us in every season of life. When God gets ready to rescue us, He sends His children to walk beside us. He always has and He always will.

I met this crazy, funny, red-head in my very first winter in the desert, but when she walked into the room it felt more like spring. Life and laughter entered the room with her. I did not have any idea who this funny lady was, but I watched with amusement as she could not sit down until she hugged every senior lady waiting to

welcome her back. Back from where, I did not know. I wondered
… *where have they been hiding this one?* She was larger than life
and I gathered that she was not a local. She seemed very
"southern". She made me smile … not only that day but every day
since. We met in the winter, but God used her to lead me into
spring. Every pastor's wife needs a friend like Denise. She makes
me laugh, encourages me, and helps me gain perspective.

The very first secret to surviving and thriving through the
seasons of life is, "Don't go it alone." We were designed for
fellowship, friendship, and faith. The Bible gives us a glimpse of
this kind of friendship in the lives of David and Jonathan. They
loved each other like brothers. David would soon be crowned king,
but before he was ready to enter into any palace, he would run for
his life and hide in caves to survive. Jonathan was there in the
winter of David's life so when spring came, David would be the
kind of king God had called him to be. A good friend always
reminds you that spring is coming when you feel encompassed in
winter.

As women, how can we walk faithfully through the seasons
of our lives? Proverbs 31:25 NIV says, *"Strength and dignity are
her clothing, and she can laugh at the days to come."* What outfit is
this lovely Proverbs 31 woman wearing? She is clothed from head
to toe with strength and dignity. How does this help her laugh no
matter what season comes her way? *"Charm is deceitful and beauty
is vain, but a woman who fears the Lord is to be praised."*
(Prov.31:30 NIV)

This book is all about what we cover ourselves with. From
swimwear to Spanx, we have pretty much tried it all. Yet, God has
the perfect covering for us. It begins with fear. Yes…we are to have
a healthy and reverent fear of God. It has been said, "We can fear
God or everything else." We are called to put on faith, hope, and
love. Fear of *everything else* can never triumph when faith, hope,
and love have us fully covered. These three will stand the test of
time. Together, we will celebrate the seasons of our lives, and we
had best not forget to laugh and dance along the way.

Don't You Look Fabulous!?!

Funny Denise. . .

How is it that the closer you get to 40, the more you wish you could dress like you're 20? I always wanted to be flashy … you know, the type that turns every guy's head when she walks in a room? That was my teenage prayer. God granted my request … he made me a six foot tall blonde with blue eyes and the 120 pound figure of a 16 year old boy. Yep, that was me … and did I ever turn heads … but not necessarily for the reason I had envisioned.

Many years ago I had the opportunity to go to a New Year's Eve celebration at what you might call an *upper crust* country club with my husband and some friends. It was the kind of night I had always dreamed of … I was going to Cinderella's ball, and I was looking for my glass slippers. We all know how that part turns out.

First on my list was the dress ... the dress *makes* the woman. I live on the border of the U.S. and Mexico, and let me tell you, the women in Mexico know how to dress-to-impress. I headed to the border town of Calexico to a swap meet which is where you get the best bargains on dresses that look like a million bucks. I found a fabulous long, dark purple, slinky dress. Just as I had anticipated, the dress was absolutely fabulous. I would turn heads like they had never been turned before.

One tiny problem ... well, two actually ... my chest was ... tiny ... and in that dress, *tiny* was a problem. So, along with my fabulous dress, the nice woman sold me what I will refer to as my "Up-lifters" to take care of my tiny problem.

The clerk demonstrated how to apply the Up-lifters on the mannequin, but something got lost in translation. I was not confident the sticky backed appliances she sold me would do the trick. In retrospect, purchasing the glue was a little bit of overkill. As it turns out, glue should never touch that particular part of a human body. Before I knew it, my fingers and chest had become one.

My husband was home at the time and I considered yelling for help, but I could not begin to explain how I got myself in this predicament. No one can successfully explain to a man the feminine mind; especially the mind of the woman who has set her sights on *fabulous!* So I spent my evening in the hot shower trying to come *unglued*, you might say.

The day had finally come and I was dying to get into my dress and strut my stuff. In addition to my Up-lifters, I had also purchased my first Spanx. This one in particular was labeled "the Spanx you can wear without clothing and look FABULOUS!!"

My new Spanx had a hook and eye closure and lifted in all the right places ... not that I would need it with the Up-lifters, but more is better, I always say! It had 25 hooks and eyes from top to

2

bottom, with an additional 3 hooks and eyes for easy access in the little girls' room. If you do the math, that is 28 prospects for disaster. Undaunted, I plunged ahead.

I pulled, tugged and sucked in as much as possible, but there was no hope I would ever get it latched without some help, so I called my husband to do his duty. He said, "Lie on the bed and let me get a good grip on those hooks." I lay down and he began what has now become a pattern in our house … the pull-tug-and-grunt ritual. He finally got it all hooked, including the three down below, and there I lay in authentic mummy fashion. He finally stopped laughing long enough to pull me up so I could commence the Up-lifters positioning.

At the store, I had also purchased some fluffy white pads to place over my miniature assets for a little additional help. *(Overkill, I embrace you as a sweet, sweet sister!)* The pads were supposed to "feel real" and would be held securely in place by the sticky Up-lifters. I positioned them carefully, removed the sticky back from the Up-lifters, boosted the little bit of bounty that nature had given me, said a prayer, and pressed hard. Everything held together, so I pulled the dress on and voila! You could have called me *chesty!*

One of my friends was a hairdresser and had come over to do my hair to resemble Reba McIntyre from the 80's while another friend did my make-up. I could have won Miss America that night. Off we went to the night of my dreams. I was Cinderella and I had my Prince. Bowing to vanity, I decided not to wear my glasses in an attempt to look even more fabulous. So, off I went, blind as a bat, but happy that I was magnificently pulled together for a night of fun, food, and fellowship with my friends.

The night started well; I was having a ball ... literally. We had a wonderful dinner, and started dancing. My husband is a great dancer … one of the many reasons I fell in love with him when we met.   About halfway through the evening I had to go to the bathroom but I wasn't worried. My husband had closed that area so quickly I had no doubt I could do it, too. (Can I just say overconfidence is not normally one of my failings?) When I finished nature's call and stood to close things up, somehow I ended up with the first hook in the second eye, the second hook in the third eye and the third hook just dangling. *Should I try again? No, I can make it through the rest of the night...I have two out of three...I'll be fine.*

Returning to join my husband at the table, I quickly realized the reason there were three hooks and three eyes, and why they all need to be properly attached. I sat down and felt a painful pinch in a most delicate area. So I stood and told my husband I wanted to dance, thinking the pinching and pain would subside if I was standing. Out to the dance floor we went, but as I took the first dance step, one of the hooks sprang with brute force away from the eye.

Oh please, don't let the last hook go, too!

I told my husband I was ready to leave but he looked at his watch and said, "OH Nooo ... you got me out here and we are staying until midnight!"

We began to dance again and everything seemed to be staying in place ... I thought. All of a sudden my husband looked at me with a smirk the size of Texas and said, "I believe your chest is rising like the sun in the East."

I looked down and those fluffy white pillows, along with the Up-lifters, were rising from the depths of the bodice of my dress. Just as I spotted this indecent exposure, the final hook and eye snapped wide open. My Spanx rolled up like a cartoon window shade and stuck out from my waist like a springboard.

There I stood with all of our community's socially elite in this fancy country club on New Year's Eve with puffy white pillows rising from my cleavage, my Uplifters dangling, and my Spanx

4

sticking straight out in front of me. Could it get any worse ... really??? I hadn't lost my glass slipper, but my dignity took a pretty good tumble.

I figured I should just laugh and keep on dancing ... life is about rolling with the punches and, in my case, dancing with the pillows. Laughter is truly the best medicine. We danced until midnight that New Year's Eve and laughed until it hurt.

Driving home, I was in a lot of pain with the unresolved hook and eye issue so I asked my husband to please try and unhook me. We pulled over into a residential neighborhood and he began to unhook the Spanx ... and, as life would have it, things got worse.

I saw flashing red and blue lights behind us and then a police officer with a flashlight tapped on my window. I rolled it down thinking; *there is no reasonable explanation for what is going on here.* He glanced at the puffy white clouds and Up-lifters rising from my chest and the Spanx protruding from my mid-section, and asked the obvious question for New Year's Eve, "Have you been drinking this evening?"

Before I could open my mouth, my husband said, "She doesn't drink. She just has floating eye hooks!"

I'd say the officer let us off with a warning, but I believe it was with a grin.

Just Debbie . . .

I understand that Denise's little adventure may have been a bit of an overshare for some of you, but you have to admit that some of the things we do in our quest for feminine beauty are just a tad over the top. Before you add Denise's name to the "Extreme Makeover" list, can you explain what is the deal with false eye lashes, Botox, tummy tucks, breast implants, nail salons, belly button piercings, Brazilian waxing and a million other crazy things that most men would never consider doing if their lives depended on it?

We just want to be *Fabulously Feminine.*

Who can forget the old movies where they would tie a corset around some poor girl before plopping her in a big ole dress to send her to the fancy ball?

Many of us thought marriage would be a lifelong dance with Prince Charming. Who doesn't start off with a romantic notion of what marriage will be like? Life is supposed to be about perfect holidays, feeling like the princess at the fancy ball, dancing the night away and living happily ever after. Perhaps your fancy ball has fallen short a few times like Denise's New Year's Eve outing? Maybe you can relate to how much work it takes these days just to make everything look like it is in the right place.

Our culture is all about glamour, wealth, and power. How can normal women begin to compare with all of the beauty that parades across our awareness each and every day? The only comforting thing is that even Cinderella lost her glass slipper ... I guess we are all happy to be in good company.

Denise's funny little story is really about two things: *the Dress* and *the Dance.* We must admit that our dress greatly affects our dance. In fact, many times in life we lose track of the dance altogether because we are more focused on the externals than our relationships.

Our family enjoyed a wonderful cruise to Alaska one summer. One of the fun things they offered each day was a dance

6

class of some kind. My teenage daughter loves to dance, so we
went to this class together. Our favorite class was Line Dancing.

I did not grow up dancing. I am very musical and love a
good rhythm, but I will be the first to admit that I *cannot* dance.
Really … truly … honestly … I am not kidding here.

I have had friends say they could teach me and they were
sure I could learn. I am just saying that anyone who was in our
class - *including my son who snuck in the back to watch and laugh
his head off* - knows I am telling the truth.

Now, don't get me wrong, I can move in an organized
fashion; I am not saying I can't move to a beat. My problem is
simply this...I am directionally impaired. I cannot differentiate left
from right, north from south, or east from west. They say things
like "step to the left … one, two, three … turn to your right" … and
on and on *and on*, ad-nauseam. These teachers who are natural
dancing machines are worse than "Simon Says" on Steroids. I am
lost as soon as they say, "Turn right."

Not only that, but why is this dancing machine of a teacher
facing the wrong direction? I have serious trouble running a credit
card through a slot in a little machine, and it's not even moving. I
can do one direction at a time if my GPS instructs me, but when it
comes to dancing; even a GPS Dance App would not help me. I
don't even win at *Twister!* It has way too many lefts, rights, overs
and unders for me. So, I must admit that when I hear the words
"Happy Dance" I have a few issues of my own because dancing
does *not* make me happy. Those watching me are more than happy,
however, they are usually cackling.

Perhaps you noticed our title was "Happy Dance" and you
have a little problem with this right from the start. Maybe you are a
lot like me and you think you can't dance. You might be thinking
that you really don't have anything to dance about, or it could be
that you don't like the first word in the title because you just don't

feel happy. This is not the season of life you want to be in right now; you don't have the finances, the job, the body, the health, or a variety of other things that you wish were yours. I get that … I truly do.

Dancing in the Bible is not about learning the Twist, the Tango, or the Two-Step. Lamentations 5:15 KJB says, *"The joy of our heart has ceased; our dance is turned into mourning."* When the people were happy, they danced. Dancing was not only an act of celebration, but it was also a component of worship.

*"Let them praise His name **in the dance**; let them sing praises unto him with the timbrel and the harp."*—Psalm 149:3 KJB. When we use the term "Happy Dance" we are simply saying that we are celebrating God in our lives with complete joy and abandon. We are no longer worried about the right foot versus the left foot; nor are we focused on ourselves or our problems. We are looking upward from our hearts in worship and celebration.

However, before the dance, comes the dress. What shall we wear? Will we need a little glue to hold it all together? I certainly hope not; that sounds pretty painful. What do we think when we look around the fancy ball?

All of these people must have perfect lives and a perfect wardrobe.

Throughout this book we will see little glimpses of the right dress for every occasion as we look at the attire of the Proverbs 31 woman. She didn't go shopping in Mexico, but the Bible tells us that she was clothed in purple and fine linens. (Prov. 31: 22) She was not held together by duct tape, glue, or Spanx. Strength and dignity adorned her.

Throughout the seasons of her life she had no fear of the snow or of the days ahead. She is remembered by this, *"Many women do noble things, but you surpass them all."* (Prov. 31:29 NIV)

This was a woman who was clothed with nobility, strength, and honor. This passage reminds us, *"Charm is deceptive, and beauty is fleeting; but a woman who fears the Lord is to be praised."* (Proverbs 31:30 NIV) Her outfit was truly timeless, as inward beauty only grows with the test of time. She lacks nothing. No wonder she can laugh at the days ahead. Just reading about her life provides a picture of a woman who loves God, is filled with wisdom and honor, and whose days are filled with service. She is always preparing for the rainy day to come. Her beauty goes way deeper than her clothing or make-up. She is fabulous, both inside and out.

When I recall Denise's story about her night at the fancy ball there is one picture I can never forget. She put it this way, "My husband looked at me with a smirk the size of Texas and said, 'I believe your chest is rising like the sun in the East'. I looked down and those fluffy white pillows, along with the Up-lifters, were rising from the depths of the bodice of my dress. Just as I spotted this indecent exposure, the final hook and eye snapped wide open. My Spanx rolled up like a cartoon window shade and stuck out from my waist like a springboard."

Those girls from the south really have a way with words that create an impression. I would like to get that picture out of my head but I just can't. It is quite the visual.

We need to be filled with the real stuff, not just uplifting fluff, if we are to be an encouragement to anyone. The Bible reminds us that our beauty is supposed to flow out of a quiet and gentle spirit. Is anyone fond of either of those words … Hmm? What does it mean to have a quiet and gentle spirit, anyway? Do we all have to be meek and mild wallflowers?

The focus in scripture is one of contentment. The Bible's idea of femininity is found in the word "submission". Our beauty is not found in being "puffed up" but in serving others.

We are reminded that *"Knowledge puffs up, while love lifts up."* (1 Corinthians 8:1 NIV) Perhaps we all need a little more of the right stuff and a little less uplifting fluff.

Ladies, remember that God has chosen the perfect outfit for you. It is extremely uplifting and will not let you down. This amazing ensemble will turn every head in the room, guaranteed. Isn't it time for all of us to get dressed and head on out to celebrate? Just let this little ensemble glide over your head; it is soft to the touch and wears well. It is attractive on every figure and takes no pliers to attach. Simply be clothed with strength, dignity, and compassion. Never leave home without it. The best covering of all time simply starts with love.

Here is the good news for all of us who feel like we just can't begin to dance. God, Himself, has sent you the invitation. He is a jealous God and He wants your very first dance. He has sent you the perfect attire, and you will be radiant wearing it. If you are anything like me, He is aware that you do not know your left from your right, and without His help you will never figure out this life on your own. But, you are not on your own. He will never leave you to figure things out alone; His hand is always waiting to guide you.

He smiles at you with love and says, "Let's dance, my daughter. Put your feet on mine. I will lead and you will follow." God, your Father, looks at you with great pride and love and simply says,

"Now, don't you look
FABULOUS!"

10

Winter … A Time to Wait

The birds are gone, the world is white,

the winds are wild, they chill and bite;

the ground is thick with slush and sleet,

and I can barely feel my feet.

The last is done, the next is here,

the same as it is every year;

spring -- then sunshine, autumn, snow,

that is how each year must go.--Author Unknown

Winter Winds …

Everything seems cold and dormant,

but spring will surely come

"See! The winter is past; the rains are over and gone."
Song of Solomon 2:11 NIV

Bunny Slopes 101

Funny Denise . . .

"Lord, I am tired of doing it my way ... just show me what you want me to do and I will do it ... let it be your will and not mine."

Have you ever prayed this prayer and as you are praying it, you just want to take it all back and say, "Just kidding God!"

It took God 12 minutes to answer my prayer. I was walking out of church that very Sunday and the youth pastor stopped me in the hallway and said, "I think you would be great at working with the high school kids."

I said, "Are you nuts?"

He said, "Nope ... I think you would be great."

My brain said, *Umm ... nope, not on your life!*

12

The next thing you know I was on my way to Big Bear as a youth sponsor for a ski retreat. I call this weekend "Bunny Slopes 101". Now here's the deal in a nutshell. I am a klutz. There are no two ways about it. I am not stable on my feet. I am 6'0" tall and have very long legs. I went into the ski shop and they gave me a pair of skis taller than me.

Really … Really … I am going to put something on my feet that will make them even longer than the size 10's I have now? I mean, I am a klutz to the 10th degree. I fall down walking from the bed to the bathroom and yet I have decided to add 6 feet of slickness to my already unstable feet? Thus began my training as a youth sponsor.

I am a weakling when it comes to body strength. To say I am not strong is a masterpiece of understatement. After putting on the many layers of clothing required for snow, I felt like a giant Pillsbury Doughboy as I reached down to put on the heaviest boots known to man. Taking my first steps in the ski boots, I looked like one of those astronauts on the moon, but with gravity … One Giant Step for Man … One Giant Nose-Dive for all the klutzes of the world.

So, off we tromped to the slopes. I laid those skis down and stepped into them with my boots. The boot latches clicked and I was suddenly tethered to danger. My entire body had gained about 50 pounds of clothing and boots, and now I was slipping and sliding over ice and snow balanced on 6 feet of slick sticks. This was a disaster waiting to happen.

One of the high school girls decided to hang with me and we were going to learn how to ski together. Another youth group sponsor decided to teach us. He showed us how to "snow plow" to stop. I practiced this technique quite a bit as I felt it was the most important thing I could possibly learn. I decided to practice this on smooth ground and located the smoothest area I could find. Problem was, the area was covered in ice … hence the glossy surface ... but I didn't realize that until I began to ski across it. To make matters worse, it was the area directly under the ski lift.

Trying to practice my snow plow, I found myself slowly sliding backwards toward the pit under the ski lift. The high school girl with me was yelling, "Just sit ... just sit down!!" Looking back, I am not sure which would have been worse ... sitting down on the ice or falling into the pit. As I sprawled on the ice with one leg forward and one behind me, skis in all directions, I thought to myself, *maybe somebody will bring me a blanket and a pillow because I am NEVER getting up.* I had no strength in my legs and I couldn't bring my skis around me. Even if I could have gotten my legs straight, I would never be able to lift myself up without first getting up onto my knees and that wasn't happening with the boots and 6 foot skis attached. I decided to take the skis off and crawl to the nearest snow bank. I was exhausted and ready to quit but our ski instructor said, "Oh no ... you need to try to ski."

I said, "Dude, I think I have skied enough to last a lifetime. I am not stupid ... I know pretty quickly when I am not good at something and will NEVER be good at this." He, however, persuaded us to get on the ski lift and head up to the Bunny Slope.

My vision of a bunny slope is a small hill where you can see the bottom from the top with one little slope in between. As we rode up the ski lift, I was enjoying the beautiful view when I suddenly became acutely aware of the passage of time and it hit me. The ski lift was not stopping to unload skiers ... it was not even slowing down. With feelings of foreboding increasing by the second, I realized that my vision of the bunny slope was sorely mistaken.

The ski lift operator was unaware that I didn't know how to ski. She was completely oblivious to the fact that I couldn't stand on skis for long periods of time, and I definitely didn't have the ability to leap off the ski lift while it was in motion. As we came closer to taking our leap of faith, I began to bellow at the ski lift operator that she was going to have to stop this ski lift in order for us to get off.

She yelled back, "I can't!"

"Well you need to slow it down!"

She repeated herself in a louder voice.

Now, if you want to talk fear, there it was. I began to watch the people ahead of us get off the chairs.

Ok ... I can do this... just lean forward and stand up. It can't be that hard ... the momentum will carry you.

As we came closer and closer to our moment of dispatch I noticed they had outlined the unloading area with orange cones.

All I have to do is stay within those orange cones and I will look like a pro! Yeah ... that's *all* I had to do ... we were next. Just as she promised, she never slowed down nor stopped the ski lift; and just as I had promised, I was not ready for what happened next.

Apparently, due to the overwhelming number of *bunnies* who refuse to get off the lift, they had implemented a drop-seat lever for easy removal of the skier. I, however, had not realized this until I saw the chair in front of me lose its seat. As fear engulfed me, I deliberated how long I would have to hold on to the bar to the right of me before that seat would pop back up under my little ski bum, because there was no way I was getting off.

As we approached the launch pad I said a prayer, "Dear God ... HELP ME!" The seat fell away and so did I. On my back, skis in the air, my legs making a wide V (that did not stand for victory) I shot across the snow wiping out each and every one of those strategically placed orange cones, coming to rest at the end of the runway. My compadre was to my left in a similar position.

15

With no other choice, I lay there spent. I couldn't get up ... I couldn't reach my skis to take them off ... I was stuck.

The ski lift operator was bellowing at me to move out of the way and I started to laugh. I had no hope of getting up; rolling over, or even crawling away ... I had nothing. Finally, she walked over, grabbed me under the arms, picked me up like a truck lift and pushed me onto the bunny slope. Rounding the corner, I saw my friend.

"Have you seen this slope? There is nothing BUNNY about it!"

I replied, "Well, we have no choice but to go, so let's suck it up and head on down."

We stood with our skis facing to the right. I offered to go first saying, "We'll zigzag all the way down the mountain (and believe me, it was a mountain), snow plow to stop at each turn, then zigzag some more. Got it?"

She gave me a deer-in-the-headlights look and nodded her head in agreement. I assumed fear's death grip was preventing audible speech at that moment. I could relate.

I shoved off to the right and snowplowed to a complete stop just short of careening over the edge into oblivion. Full of my initial success, I proudly turned to her saying, "Just follow my lead." I lifted my left ski and planted it facing left. I lifted my right ski and began to slalom ... not my original intent ... one leg on the ground and one leg wagging behind me, the ski repeatedly banging me on the head. This amazing spectacle lasted for about 30 feet before I fell and continued to roll for a while. When my momentum finally slowed to a stop, I raised my head to see skiers zipping past, dodging my body. I closed my eyes and sought my happy place.

My ski buddy didn't even try to move; she just sat there a few feet above me, dazed and staring into space. We had all we could stand. At some unspoken signal, we removed our skis, stood up, raised our chins, gathered our tattered pride and took the high road as we WALKED down the bunny slope.

A half hour later we were drinking hot chocolate and sitting by a fireplace. I must admit, it was a bonding moment. From then on we would laugh uproariously at the mention of snow, skis, and bunny slopes. This was my humble beginning as a youth sponsor.

Just Debbie ...

Has there ever been a time in your life when, like Denise, you were excited about your new area of ministry, but before the excitement could even wear off, you found yourself on the bunny slopes, and it was not at all what you had in mind? Wasn't your new ministry supposed to be fulfilling, encouraging, and stimulating to your heart, soul, and mind?

What kind of things can we learn on the bunny slopes of life? Let's just review Denise's interesting day and the lessons she learned in "Bunny Slopes 101":

1) She prayed and asked God to clearly reveal how she could serve Him.
2) She was invited to be a youth sponsor, which included a youth group ski trip.
3) Her day started with a challenge and skis that were bigger than she could handle.
4) She realized her own strength was limited.

17

5) The Bunny Slope looked a lot more like a mountain than a bunny hill.

6) She discovered the bottom can literally fall right out from under you.

7) As she approached the drop zone she prayed, "Help Me God!"

8) She learned what it is like to fall and need help to get back up again.

9) Feeling discouraged, cold, and shaken, Denise was ready to give up.

10) Realizing she couldn't make it on her own, she found support to walk down the hill.

Now I ask you, does any of this sound familiar or similar to anything you have read in the Bible? Before God can MAKE us, He has to BREAK us.

How much better could Denise learn to serve as a youth sponsor than to understand through her own experience how a young person feels? The challenges they face are new and untried; life can seem strange as they find their way on unfamiliar footings. They are bound to fall at some time, and they are going to need someone to understand who will help them get back up again, without judging. Their bunny hills feel like mountains to them. They will need someone to help them when they cry out for help, and to walk beside them when they are ready to quit because they feel like a failure. It appears that Denise had more than one instructor guiding her that day.

Without winter there would be no spring. None of us like the cold, dismal, dormancy that comes after the snow is gone when the chill winds remain and the earth looks dead and desolate. Shakespeare's famous words seem to capture it nicely, *"Now is the winter of our discontent."* Our discontent with winter has to do with perseverance; that is the center of our difficulty because winter is the time of waiting.

Song of Solomon 2:11-12 NASB says, *"For behold the winter is past, the rain is over and gone. The flowers have already appeared in the land; the time has arrived for pruning the vines."*

We need to see that every season serves a purpose in God's master plan.

I live in sunny California where there are amazing vineyards. Each week, through communion, we partake of the fruit of the vine. I have always marveled at how Jesus used this picture to catch our attention when he said, *"This is my blood."*

I think a cup of wine is a picture of beauty, but I must admit I really had very little understanding of how the process works until a recent visit to a vineyard where I learned a little bit about the annual growth cycle of the grape vines. The process of spring begins with a bud break. If the vine has been pruned during winter, the start of this cycle is signaled by a "bleeding" of the vine. *Wow, that's an interesting word for them to use!*

Bleeding occurs when the soil begins to warm and osmotic forces push water, organic acids, hormones, minerals, and sugars up from the root system of the vine. It is expelled from the cuts or "wounds" left from pruning the vines. During this period, a single vine can bleed up to five liters.

So, are they still talking about grapevines or did they just start talking about people? Have you ever wondered what the *dark season of winter* is accomplishing in your life? It seems so long, cold, and dormant. It is during the pruning or cleaning, as the Greek puts it, that there is bleeding. These cuts are the pathway to new growth.

Do you ever feel like a grape that is being stomped? Sometimes I feel more like a raisin, but you know what I mean. Let's look at what our heavenly Father, the gardener, has to say about the pruning process in our lives:

19

"I am the true vine, and my Father is the gardener. ² He cuts off every branch in me that bears no fruit, while every branch that does bear fruit he prunes so that it will be even more fruitful. ³ You are already clean because of the word I have spoken to you. ⁴Remain in me, as I also remain in you. No branch can bear fruit by itself; it must remain in the vine. Neither can you bear fruit unless you remain in me." (John 15:1-4 NIV)

What is God's purpose in pruning us, humbling us, and allowing our hearts to be broken? John 15: 11-13 NIV says, *"I have told you this so that my joy may be in you and that your joy may be complete. ¹² My command is this: Love each other as I have loved you. ¹³ Greater love has no one than this, than to lay down one's life for one's friends."*

When winter comes and God is pruning us, everything seems dormant. When we feel like the life has been sucked out of us, just wait for it. As surely as winter comes, there will be spring. There will be new life.

Just as the grape vines bleed before they bloom and grow to produce the fruit to be made into new wine, we may feel just like a big old grape, stomped and bleeding. But what is the new wine mentioned here? What is it we are to produce after we are pruned? What will make our Father's joy complete? Loving each other as He has loved us makes us a reflection of Him.

Is it any wonder that conflict is often at the center of the dark night of our winter? God uses winter to help us bear new fruit, and that fruit is love. Do you have a relationship that needs healing? Does it feel like someone has taken clipping sheers to your heart? Have you ever felt like your heart is bleeding and torn? We need to understand and remember that God has a purpose in every season.

It may feel like winter now, but if you allow God to prune and clean away the old you, it won't be long at all until you see new, productive growth. The next time you cringe when the cold winds blow right through you or you feel the pain of pruning in your life, remember that we are becoming new wine, and must let go of the old whine.

When God is getting ready to use you to minister to others and to love others in His name, He will certainly bring you through a little learning experience of your very own. When that happens, try Denise's prayer, "*Lord, I am tired of doing it my way. Just show me what you want me to do and I will do it . . . let it be your will and not mine.*" Then try not to take your words back. Instead, wait and see the new thing that God will do in your life. You will find yourself skiing again before you know it. You may even look back at the important lessons learned while on the bunny slopes because you have moved on up the hill.

The greatest lessons of winter are often learned on "Bunny Slopes 101".

Spring … *A Time to Plant*

"The fields are rich with daffodils,
A coat of clover cloaks the hills,
And I must dance, and I must sing
To see the beauty of the spring."

--Author Unknown

Spring Beginnings …

Everything comes alive with the beauty of the creator.

April showers bring May flowers.

"There is a time for everything, and a season for every activity
under the heavens."—Ecclesiastes 3:1 NIV

The Spanx Attack

Funny Denise …

What is it about Easter morning that the birds seem to be singing more sweetly, the flowers seem to be more colorful, and the sun seems to be shining brighter? For many years my husband and I have chosen to get up before sunrise on Easter morning, stand out in the middle of the street facing east with coffee and hot chocolate in hand to watch the sunrise together. It's brilliant … it's soothing … it's a promise from God on so many levels … and this Easter was no exception.

It was Sunday morning; we had seen the sunrise and were getting ready for church. I couldn't wait for Easter Sunday this year as I had bought a beautiful Easter dress. It was lovely with brilliant

23

greens, yellows, and blues. The dress had a V-neck collar and was a tad on the short side ... at least for me. The belt tied at the waist above a beautifully flared skirt.

I had bought the dress a month earlier but as I put it on I realized that, apparently, a month earlier I had been starving myself. Sometime during the time between my purchase and this Easter morning, I had come to my senses and put on all the weight I had lost in the previous six months. The belt was supposed to be tied in a bow, but there was just enough length to tie a knot, at best. This Easter I was determined to look fabulous if it was the last thing I ever did.

I went to my drawer-of-wonders to pull out the fix-it item of the day. I laid out three possibilities to choose from...my wonder-Spanx. I *wonder* how to get them on, I *wonder* if my body will remain in them, and I *wonder* if I will ever get them off.

My drawer-of-wonders is filled with all shapes and sizes ... I have the *I-sort-of-feel-chunky-Spanx* that wraps only around my mid-section just below my bust. I have the *I-went-to-bed-with-one-roll-and-woke-up-with-two-Spanx* that snugly covers my growing torso. Last, I have the *I-went-to-bed-as-a-20-year-old-and-woke-up-as–a-50-year-old-with-nothing-in-the–right-spot-Spanx* that goes from over the shoulders, covers small boulders and reaches to my knees ... my favorite. I buy them all in black as my mother always told me that black covers a multitude of sins and the older I get, the bigger the multitude. This Easter morning I needed help ... I had to bring out the big guns.

Now getting into this kind of contraption takes a lot of encouragement. I have to encourage my husband to keep pulling, even when he believes there is no hope of cramming all of my bounty into that small area. After at least five minutes of him pulling and tugging and me jumping and wiggling, I was finally in ... it was a miracle but we did it ... and then ... well ... nature called. Now, they make these things with openings for just such an

24

occasion so this shouldn't have been an issue … IF I had remembered not to put underwear on before the Spanx … oops!

Back came my husband to pull and tug some more. In the midst of our tug-of-Spanx, I asked him why he stood so far away from me as he was pulling and tugging, and he said, "Hun … ya know I love ya right? But when I help you on and off with these things I am afraid that I am going to get slapped by your belly or your booty." I wanted to tell him he was in danger of getting slapped, but not by those particular body parts.

After 15 minutes of pulling and tugging I was finally loaded and ready for my dress, but my legs looked really white so I located a pair of panty hose and pulled them on over the Spanx. I finally put on the dress and heels and off we went to church.

I felt like a million bucks as I walked across the parking lot to the sanctuary. As we walked into the church and up the aisle, though, I realized that my dress had developed an inordinate amount of static electricity and was clinging to my hose, Spanx, and legs.

Well this won't work! So I headed to the bathroom. I figured the static electricity was from my panty hose so I raced into the bathroom and removed the panty hose only to discover it was the Spanx. I needed to remove the SPANX; and so began the process of taking the dress off and removing the armor … by myself.

After another 10 minutes, dripping in sweat, I finally had the hose off, the Spanx off, and the dress back on when it hit me … my purse was at the front of the church, third pew on the right. What would I do with the undergarments in my hand? I came out of the bathroom with both items in hand and spotted my husband. I asked him to go get my purse and he said, "No way … just put them somewhere in the bathroom."

Good idea! So back to the bathroom I went. *Where, oh where can I hide them? Ahhhhh, the wicker couch . . . I can stick them under the cushion. Nobody will see them ... I can get them after church ... life is grand!*

I rejoined my husband looking like the cat that ate the canary and up the aisle I went. However, as I walked I realized the dress still had static, but now I had on *no undergarments!*

When the service was over, all I wanted to do was grab my stuff and run ... but as luck would have it, it was my day to teach children's church. I decided to grab the goods, put them on and not worry about the static electricity. It was time for our drama sketch and I needed to make it quick. Today had already been filled with more drama than we had rehearsed.

When I walked back into the bathroom there were two ladies sitting on the wicker couch breast feeding their babies. There's really no easy way to say, "Excuse me ladies but I believe your cheeks are sitting on my Spanx ... could you please move them?" So I decided to teach Children's Church in all my glory hoping the only ones that would know I was without my physical armor would be God and me.

Finally, it was time to go home. I raced to the bathroom to find those same two women still sitting on the wicker sofa chit chatting, but I wasn't leaving without my Spanx. I politely informed them church was over and I was certain their spouses were waiting on them to go to lunch. I grabbed those garments and high-tailed it out to the car. I wish I could tell you what the sermon was about that day but my biggest concern was my undergarments ... or lack thereof.

This glorious Easter morning had started out with such promise. As I drove home I couldn't help but wonder what had gone wrong. Just hours before, I had stood watching the Easter sunrise with my cup of hot chocolate, ready to celebrate Jesus' resurrection. Now I had to admit the message of Easter had totally passed me by.

I meant well. Perhaps you can relate? Perhaps you, too, have felt the breeze of uncertainty blowing through your exposed underpinnings? Alright maybe I am the only one who has felt that many breezes on Easter morning, but you know what I mean.

You know, I think I actually might have learned a little more that Easter than I first thought. My desire has always been to walk in God's glory, not my own, and I began to think about how important it is in life to be properly covered. All I could think about that day was Spanx, Spanx, Spanx. I had allowed my mind to be consumed by the physical instead of focusing on the spiritual and I missed the message of Easter as a result. So, remember what your mama always told you and never leave home without putting on your armor.

Just Debbie . . .

The message of Easter is that Jesus Christ defeated death, and the enemy no longer has a hold over us. How many times have we read that, even though Christ defeated death, we still need to put on the armor of God? The problem is that I have never served in battle - at least, not an earthly battle - and I have a hard time relating to putting on body armor. So, guess what word picture God brought to my mind? Oh yeah, you got it ... every girl needs her body armor, right?

That Easter had begun for Denise with tying that belt around her waist and donning her physical armor. But when a little static hit, she took that garment off and hid it under the nearest cushion. After hearing about her difficulties, I must admit that I began to see Ephesians from a little different perspective. You might also have a whole new visual of putting on your armor. God's Word for us is to "*Be strong in the Lord and in his mighty power.*" (Ephesians 6:10 NIV)

We really can't afford to leave off our *Spiritual Spanx* in this life. When we do, we are exposed and vulnerable in all of our glory versus standing in His glory. Ephesians 6 reminds us that every day we are going to face some real life challenges. The devil's scheme is to attack us and make us think our struggle is with other people.

When we are feeling vulnerable and kind of out there, we are thinking that our problem is with the person who is driving us crazy at work, the slow unpredictable driver ahead, or the two women on the wicker couch who just keep sitting and talking. We are convinced that we need someone else to change or move out of our way before we can be happy.

This passage goes on to tell us that we need a few more things to complete our beautiful Easter ensemble. We need some beautiful shoes to keep us walking in peace. Every day we have the choice to either be offended or take the high ground. We can focus on the person who let us down or we can be strong in God's mighty power. We can react with impatience, anger, or even revenge, or we can realize that God promises to meet all of our needs even when people let us down. Now these shoes are made for walking!

One last thing we must not leave home without is our purse. The next time you are holding that cute little purse tucked tightly in your arms, remember that we are to take up our shield of faith every day so we can extinguish all the flaming arrows that will come our way.

What is it that is so wonderfully promising about Easter? All the fullness of spring culminates in this one day as we celebrate new life, new hope, and new beginnings. Death is defeated and the victory is ours. Spring is central to all of the other seasons. It is the time of planting that comes after the long season of dormancy. Summer is the time where the heat bears down and brings forth ripening growth. Autumn is the time of harvest and the changes in color that eventually lead to death and waiting. Waiting for what? Spring ... oh glorious spring!

Without the Resurrection we would have no hope. Our victory is centered in this most glorious and powerful of seasons. While the victory has already been won, the battle still rages.

The enemy is just waiting to find us weak, vulnerable, and naked without our protective covering. Many of us just want to escape at the first sign of testing or discomfort, and some of us are running around without ever putting God's armor on in the first place.

Ephesians 6 gives us an in-depth look at the kind of covering we need to wear each and every day if we are going to be women of nobility in this life. I have heard many teachings that have examined all of the military parts of God's armor such as the breastplate of righteousness, the belt of truth, and feet that are fitted with the gospel of peace. In addition, there is the shield of faith, the helmet of salvation, and the sword of the Spirit. I now have realized that I may have missed the meaning and importance of this message because I just couldn't relate to a military description. It seemed so masculine ... so not me.

When Denise began talking about all the ways that we try to cover ourselves, smooth ourselves, and make ourselves conform to be presentable in public, it hit me ... this military sounding armor is not just for men. Women need to be protected from all the attacks that come our way, too. I now have a picture of Spanx that I can't get out of my mind no matter how hard I try. I know many of the theologians are rolling their eyes right now - but a lot of them are men.

I know this visual of Spanx is a stretch, but then it *is* made out of Lycra, so bear with me, please. We would never leave our homes without all of our essential undergarments in place, but we often leave home without giving God much attention, time, study, or prayer to get us safely through our day, spiritually. When the first obstacle comes our way we are left vulnerable and open to defeat.

Look for just a moment at what the armor of God does for us. Here are some descriptions of the functions this armor provides in our lives: (taken from Eph.6: 10-12)

- It is strong and gives us mighty power.
- It helps us to stand firm against the enemy.
- We not only look fabulous but, protected with God's armor, we can be fearless.

Are you facing any attacks in your life? They can come at us many different ways: conflict, sickness, suffering, persecution, addictions, unfairness, prejudice, cruelty ... just to name a few. This passage reminds us, however, that our battle is not about people or powers in this world.

The next time you find yourself wondering how to make it through your day, be sure to put on your Spiritual Spanx. This protective garment will make you fabulous, fearless, and faithful; one size fits all. There is no way to successfully stand throughout the seasons of life without God's protection and power. You can call it your armor, your Spanx, or your Proverbs 31 covering. Whatever you choose to call it, you had best not leave home without it if you want to be victorious.

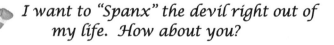

I want to "Spanx" the devil right out of my life. How about you?

30

Summer … A Time to Love

The earth is warm, the sun's ablaze,
It is a time of carefree days;
And bees abuzz that chance to pass
May see me snoozing in the grass.
—Author Unknown

Summer Heat Waves …

Everything placed in the fire is purified,

And refined as gold.

"For day and night your hand was heavy upon me;
my strength was sapped as in the heat of summer."

—Psalm 32:4 NIV

31

"It's A Climb"

Funny Denise...

There are basically five kinds of swimsuits for the seasons in a woman's life: the Bikini, the Tankini, the Trunkini, the Tentini and the Longitini. Let me elaborate ...

First you have the bikini to show off what your mama gave you. It can come in a multitude of colors, designs, and most likely will have strings. My first bikini was a cute little red polka-dot number. I bought it and was promptly caught trying it on by my mother. She told me that if I could prance in front of my father wearing that string bikini I could prance on the beach. I really wanted that bikini, but I am not stupid. So that night I timed it perfectly. I waited until my Dad was seated in his recliner, newspaper perched in front of him with the TV blaring and the discernible onset of his rumbling snores. I promptly walked through the family room and did a pirouette in front of my dad, held my hands out to show him the entire swim suit, and marched into the kitchen to tell my mother I had showed it to my father.

She asked what he said and I replied, "Nothing negative."
As Mom went flying into the family room, I went flying out the
door and off to the beach.

At the age of 18 our body parts are still in the general
vicinity of where they should be. In your thirties, after having
children, most women resort to the Tankini. The Tankini covers the
mid-section that, for some reason or another, has become less perky
and more abundant.

Mid-life finds us shopping for what we call the Trunkini.
The Trunkini is a Tankini with ruffles. The Trunkini was developed
for those of us who normally wear Spanx on a daily basis to keep
our abundance in place. Basically the word "Trunk" says it all.
Everything is locked in the trunk and it is really better for everyone
on the beach if it stays there. A Trunkini is the menopausal
woman's best beach companion.

This is the precursor to the Tentini. This suit comes
complete with a built in porta-potty, storage compartment, and
enough room that you can camp out for days. It is the Moo-Moo of
the islands. It will not attract men, but people will flock to you to
enjoy the shade.

At this point in my life I am weary of fighting the Battle of
the Bulge. To tell you the truth, I do not consider myself old
enough to wear any of this military action. Anything that begins
with a Trunk or a Tank is just way to boot-campish for me.

Another excellent choice for the mature woman is to
become a Longitini girl. These suits are made entirely of Spandex
and are perfect for the woman who is more longitudinally
challenged. Those ladies who find that everything is migrating
south, and describe their bra as a *36-Long*, fit nicely into this last
group. It is no accident if this sounds vaguely similar to one of my
other favorite things ... Spanx. Oh yes, I feel better already. This
suit is the miracle of its day. It stretches from the north to the south

and the east to the west. The Lycra takes what hangs low and lifts it up; the Spandex takes what bulges out and sucks it in. It offers the modern, mature girl everything she needs to revisit the pool with confidence, if not style.

As they say in Real Estate . . . location, location, location! Girls, trust me, this suit is where it's at. This little miracle suit relocates, lifts and tucks everything in. Now there is no need to cry when it is time to trade in your Speedo. You may not be able to breathe, but you can always pretend that you were just out for a run if someone shows concern over any panting, gasping or wheezing that might escape your lips.

While we are having true confessions of the soul, as much as it pains me to admit it, my bikini days are long, long gone. Perhaps they should never have been here to begin with, but my daddy was sleeping in his chair when I asked for permission. So, that is all water under the bridge. I will not begin to cover the topic of a bikini in this story as a bikini cannot begin to cover me.

The closest I have come recently to wearing something like that is the day I tried-on a thong. For some of you well-seasoned gals, I am not describing mere beach attire. When we were growing up, a thong referred to the sandals or flip flops that adorned our cute little feet every summer. I assure you that *The Thong* for the new generation is a whole different animal. Before you start diagnosing me with a mid-life crisis or something worse, let me just assure you that I did not choose my thong. No ... this little secret belonging to Victoria was thrust upon me in a most unusual way.

I make it no secret that my favorite perfume of all time is sold only at Victoria's Secret. I love this delicate perfume and request it each year for Christmas. It gives my husband a gift idea for me that surpass the usual broom, appliance or tool of his choosing. The problem arose one year at Christmas when his dear little southern mama was here for the holidays and they went shopping together.

34

Now I ask you, seriously, what kind of life is there after the devastation that occurs when you put on a thong and *can no longer find it*? There is only one recourse ... DIET!

I have spent my entire life trying to come up with ways to lose weight other than eating fruits and vegetables and/or exercising. I am a firm believer that eating anything resembling the front yard cannot, and will not ever be good for you. All my life I have avoided green vegetables. I find no use for them and have absolutely no idea how to prepare them.

Looking back, I remember the first year I was married to my husband and he wanted a healthy snack. He said, "I bought some broccoli and it's in the refrigerator. Can you prepare it and bring it to me with some ranch dip?" To which he added, "Make sure you cut the stalks off."

I went to the kitchen and cut the stalks off, placed the broccoli on a plate with the ranch dip and took it to him like a good wife of one year.

He looked at the plate, looked at me and said, "Baby, where is the broccoli?"

I said, "It's right there in front of you on the plate."

He said, "Um, Hun ... you just gave me the stalks."

I said, "Well you didn't want to eat that bush thingy did you, because I threw that part away." I mean, who wants to eat something that looks like part of your front yard? Since then I have been told that broccoli is the intestinal scrub brush for the human body. Now I ask you, does that sound pleasant at all?

Every January I start a new diet. It starts the first day I pour myself into my work clothes and waddle off to work following the overindulgence of the Christmas holidays. I need to find a diet where I can eat bread, pasta, chocolate, and any meat except fish. It also needs to exclude vegetables, fruits, and some funky thing called tofu (gag!) My idea of vegetables is French fries. They are small and shaped a lot like carrot sticks. Coming from Texas has helped me devise my own food pyramid. *Fried* is a major food group there. I truly believe that if you eat enough fried foods they will slide in and out of you before you know it. I might add that I have yet to convince anyone of my ideas on diet plans.

Going to a gym is another story, and an experience in itself. Have you ever walked into a gym and not known how to use the machines? You stand in front of these masochistic monstrosities and pretend you are stretching until you can try and figure them out. I decided to get on an elliptical climber. How hard could it be? It's like skiing, right?

I stepped up on the climber just like any professional and began to "ski". I ... looked ... goooood! 10 minutes later I realized the machine wasn't on when the man next to me pointed at the controls above the handles and said, "You need to turn it on."

Being college educated, I found the big green button with the word ON and pushed it, but there were so many buttons ... so many choices to make. I was embarrassed, so I just hit the first button I saw, quickly realizing that the man next to me was snickering. (I promptly dubbed him the *Gym Snob* or *Exer-Geek* ... but I digress ...) I had apparently pushed the button for Alps climbing, and at Level 10 it was taking me approximately a minute per step.

He leaned over to me and said, "Did you mean to push those buttons? Well good luck with that and I hope you make the 30 minutes you set the timer for." (Confirmed ... Gym Snob!)

As sweat was pouring from my face and body I thought to myself ... *I can do this ... I can do this, at least until he gets off and he won't see me leave.* He climbed for the next 29 minutes just out of spite. I won't share my ensuing thoughts ...

It is difficult enough to begin this whole exercise thing, but when you get home you want to reward yourself for being such a good girl. The whole concept of eating things with bright colors is just wrong on so many levels. If you ask me, things that are green and red belong on a Christmas tree; they do not belong in a small stomach that can swell like a pumpkin. Not only do they want you to eat raw, crunchy things but then they ask you to wash it down with a barrel of water. Before you know it, your stomach is imitating a washing machine on the large load, extra spin cycle ... not at all pleasant.

There is summertime, swimsuits, diet, and exercise ... what's a girl to do? We only wish those polka-dot bikini days would find us again.

Just Debbie ...

"Dear God, I feel fat again. Please, help me!"

Oh please, don't tell me you have never prayed this secret little prayer. I grant you this is not a Sunday morning service kind of prayer. No, this is a true closet prayer. We pray it after we walk in there and find nothing to wear. We had good intentions, but we love our fast food, and now we need a fast fix. This little prayer starts right after a long winter of cozy sweaters, yoga pants, comfort foods, and lots of hot chocolate. Then the papers have the nerve to start advertising the latest summer swimsuits, and vacation time is just around the corner.

Just for one minute, let's be refreshingly honest and admit that most of us have spent more prayer time in our closets worrying about what we will wear, how we will look, and how we feel about ourselves than truly praying about what God sees inside us.

Why is this? Perhaps we have listened for years to people say things like, "The suit makes the man." So does it also follow that the swimsuit makes the girl? Society bombards us with it and objectifies us in it. *Sports Illustrated* dedicates an entire issue to the swimsuit every year. (Speaking of objectifies ...!) I think the swimsuit represents our *Catch 22*; we are more worried about how we look in it rather than whether it will stay in place while we are swimming those laps every day.

Well, girls, let's just be painfully honest here. The least of our problems as women is with our teeny weenie polka-dot bikinis. We all wish those were the only decisions we were making today. Our decisions are more about downhill slides and upward climbs. My daughter loves the Miley Cyrus song, "It's a Climb". When it comes to getting the areas of our lives in order, that's pretty much the bottom line, it *IS* a climb.

The Apostle Paul makes me feel a little bit better when he says that he does the things he doesn't want to do, and there are also times when he doesn't do the things he should. That pretty well sums us up, and I am betting that might be your life story too.

Here is the root of our problem. Very simply put, we often don't like what is good for us. It is an acquired taste and many of us don't want to acquire it; we would rather settle for the cheap substitute. There is a slogan for a soda that says, "It's the REAL THING!" The funny thing is that it isn't the real thing at all; it is an artificially flavored, sugary substitute for water.

All of my favorite summer memories involve WATER. I love the water. When it comes to summer, just give me water ... lots and lots of clear blue, refreshingly cool water. I want to sit by it, swim in it and gaze at it. I love to watch the fireworks over the bay, and I love to float down the lazy river. There is only one problem. Although I love to swim in water, I really can't stand to drink it. I could live on sweet iced tea, but I don't like the real deal. Drinking enough water is a major struggle of my life.

Have you ever been dehydrated? Well, I have pretty much lived my life that way, and it's not wise when living in the desert. One day I had been in the pool and was feeling no pain. I was actually quite cool and comfy. I decided to hop on my bike and ride to a friend's house. Off I pedaled with my little water bottle. It was only a few miles away, but it was a triple digit day.

The problem started when my swimsuit dried, then my water bottle ran out, and I was pedaling uphill with a ways to go. My legs started shaking, and soon my body joined in. I knew I needed water and fast. I looked in front of me and saw an apartment complex right on the corner of the street and there was a pool. With legs and arms shaking I climbed the fence and jumped in, clothes and all. The people there stared at me with fear and reverence. Never get in the way of a truly thirsty person because they mean business.

Jeremiah 2:13 NIV says, *"My people have committed two sins: They have forsaken me, the spring of living water, and have dug their own cisterns, broken cisterns that cannot hold water."*

Do you see the problem? These people were not thirsty for the living water. They were digging for substitutes; they had "dug their own cisterns" by worshipping other gods. These were the cheap imitations for the real thing.

Not only were we designed to need water, we were designed to be filled with the springs of living water. Many of us reach for a sugary drink instead of water, and I am pretty sure we do the same thing in our spiritual walk with God. We settle for substitutes: wealth, power, sex, approval, beauty, careers ... the list of things we idolize goes on and on. God calls this sin. It will not only leave us weak, it will leave us empty and craving the wrong things.

One key word for summer survival is *hydration*. We will never survive the heat of summer without it. Staying hydrated spiritually is one struggle we all face. Choosing to be healthy is another huge leap. I think many of us can relate to struggling with the diet mentality, as well. There are more fad diets these days than there are fast food restaurants; the faster the fix, the more popular the diet. We love the commercials that tell us we can have our cake and eat it too.

Let's be really honest here ... fad diets don't work because they are temporary solutions to a permanent issue. We need permanent life changes; changes in our minds, our souls, and our bodies. If you don't like to eat green and red, or you hate to drink water and exercise, how will you make any progress? I guess we could just hide out in our Tentini's, but hiding does not solve the problem.

2 Timothy 1:7 NLT says, *"For God has not given us a spirit of fear, but of power, love, and self-discipline."* Here is the bad news: I don't have the strength or the desire to change on my own...nope, nada, don't have it, not gonna happen. The good news is: God will give us a spirit of power, love and self-discipline. He doesn't give a lifetime supply all at once. He gives strength for each day as we ask.

For some of us, at first this may not sound like good news. Why do we have to ask every day for our daily bread? He already knows we need it. Why can't we ask once and then receive it for life?

God wants us to ask Him for strength each day so He can teach us to walk side-by-side with him and draw closer to him; so we can learn to hear and recognize His voice. It is about building a relationship with him. If you were trying to build a relationship with someone else, would you tell them once that you love them and then never talk to them again, or only when you needed something? Just like a diet or an exercise program, learning to walk step-by-step with Christ every day is a discipline, well worth the effort to learn. If you do, you'll realize you have never felt so loved.

That, my friends, is good news for any closet pray-er. The question is, "Will we be prepared for the challenges of the future if we continue with the same attitudes, actions, and choices we are making today?

The Proverbs 31 woman was called virtuous because she was prepared. Each day we can choose life, and we can choose how to live life. While God has our days numbered, we get to choose how we live life day-by-day. Many of us make short-term resolutions but forget that we need changes for a lifetime when the summer heat hits physically, spiritually, and emotionally.

We have two available choices: a "downward slide" or an "uphill climb". We dare not wait for a sunny day, a perfect day, or a day that we feel good enough. All of our tomorrows are based on the decisions we make today.

The pain will be worth the gain, but make no mistake, it's a Climb.

Fall … A Time to Change

The leaves are yellow, red, and brown,
A shower sprinkles softly down;
The air is fragrant, crisp, and cool,
And once again I'm stuck in school.

--Author Unknown

Autumn Changes …

Nothing stays the same;

Everything in life changes

"As long as the earth endures, seedtime and harvest, cold and heat,
summer and winter, day and night will never cease."
—Genesis 8:22NIV

Just Nuke Me Now!

Just Debbie

Do you remember those wonderful days of Global Warming debates? Al Gore traveled the globe sounding the battle cry. Everyone was asking questions like, "Do humans impact climate change? How can we better calculate emissions? How can we 'go green' and leave a better footprint on this world we live in?"

Now the problem with this debate is that all practical good sense was thrown out the window. Helloooo ... any woman at that special stage of life can tell you that her personal *climate changes* affect everyone in her house when she has one simple little Hot Flash.

The Global Warming people tell us to calculate emissions to see how we are affecting the world. Really? Do they seriously want us to calculate how much moisture can come out of the female body as her insides heat up like a microwave on full power nuking a small donut? You know how a microwave has the partial power

43

button? Not us, baby, it is all or nothing! The full power button kicks on and that poor little donut is … well … toast.

We are also told how global warming leaves a "footprint" on the world. Do these same individuals not remember the kind of footprints we leave if someone gets in our way when the volcano is ready to blow? While the world's mantra is all about Global Warming, the female battle cry is "Just Nuke Me Now!"

As women, our lives are filled with seasons. I like to compare these seasons to Denise's style of cooking. There is nuking, frying, burning, and spontaneous combustion. This last method of cooking is what happens when the inside of something gets so hot it explodes from the inside out. This, my friends, is my view of menopause. If you have not yet had the experience … as with global warming, just wait for it. Don't be too smug because your day will come and there is no way to prepare for this little internal climate change.

Every season of a woman's life is filled with miscellaneous "girl things". You know what we are talking about … diapers, bras, feminine products, breast pumps, Spanx, and then Depends. This is just our equipment to stay in the game. Now, add PMS, hot flashes, night sweats, hormone imbalances and mood swings, and you have a recipe for disaster. It's a wonder we make it through.

If you were lucky, your mom told you about puberty and prepared you for that "special time of the month." Hopefully, she was also there for you through delivering and raising your children. Yet, I would be willing to bet she forgot to discuss that one major life-changing event that can cause you to strip off your clothes in the most inappropriate places, promotes creativity in making fans out of the most unusual items, and can make you look forward to unexpected outbursts directed at the most docile individual just because they are standing in front of you.

44

They call it menopause and we all get it if we live long enough, whether we are ready for it or not ... and we are *never* ready for it. If you are tired of your man asking if you have PMS, are just plain crazy, or if you are in menopause, I suggest you just go with *global warming* as a handy response. After all, it worked for good old Al, right?

Funny Denise...

Menopause assaulted my "temple" 18 months after my hysterectomy at the age of 39. To say the least, I was ecstatic about never again having my "monthly visitor" until one frightful day in January.

There I sat in a presentation meeting amidst all of the attorneys I worked for. I began to feel irritable, then angry, and then the back of my neck began to leak. Not only did my neck leak but places on my body that should never secrete fluid began to drip. I mean, whose body drips sweat from inside their elbow or the backs of their knees? When it was all said and done, I was soaking wet, flushed at radioactive level, and angrier than a wet hen. I suddenly remembered my doctor saying I might start experiencing hot flashes soon after my hysterectomy.

Well thank you, God, that hot flash thingy is over with and I won't have to deal with that ever again!

Half an hour later, I was being nuked alive ... again.

Fast forward to August, four years later; my hot flashes had become as regular as clockwork and hit about every hour, if not sooner. I was learning to live with them as best I could, and my husband had become quite adept at taking cover when he saw the flush rising in my cheeks. It was a work in progress but we were learning to cope.

My husband and I had gone to the video store to get a stack of movies. Our plan was to settle down in our air conditioned home that Friday night in August and not emerge until Sunday morning for church. Standing in the checkout line, I felt the microwave engage. I looked at my husband and he flinched. His look said *I want to bolt out of the store before you totally embarrass me.*

My look said, *if I had a sharp object I could hurt somebody here!* I glanced at the clerk and - apparently - verbalized my thought, "Did they hire this guy from the DMV because he is slower than molasses." My husband shrunk down behind the candy aisle and began closely scrutinizing the ingredients in each and every candy bar on the shelf.

The lady in front of me turned quickly away with a look of fear when she saw the sweat pouring down my face as I wiped and slung sweat off my arms. The man behind me backed away slowly, switched lines, and began motioning for those behind him to take cover.

I finally got to the counter and gave my videos to the clerk. He must have been no older than 16. He smiled and took my movies. I felt my husband touch my shoulder as if he were gentling a skittish colt ... *Easy gal ... Easyyy ...* And there it was ... I spotted it across the counter, against the back wall ... a FAN! I was so excited! I politely asked the young clerk if that fan worked. He smiled and shrugged his shoulders. I said, "Hun," (southern jargon, typically used before leaping across the counter to strangle the clerk) "could you please plug it in and see if it works?" He shrugged his shoulders and kept ringing up the videos. My voice took on a Zuul-like timbre and crazed urgency similar to the one your mama used when you were on her ever-lovin' last nerve

46

(thinking back on it now, she was probably menopausal, too) ... and I said, "PLUG IT IN AND DO IT NOW!!"

I heard the candy rack fall over and watched my husband trying to hide under the gummy bear boxes. The clerk turned around and plugged the fan in, and believe it or not ... pointed it directly at *himself.* I kid you not, the man in the other line looked at the clerk and said, "Listen son ... you have no idea what you're messing with ... turn that fan on this woman and back slowly away ... it's for your own good!"

The clerk pointed the fan at me and I pulled my collar down to get air in the general vicinity of the leakage. All the men took another step back. Soon the hot flash subsided and I looked at the clerk and said, "You ok? Are you finished with my transaction?"

"Yes ma'am," he faltered, before asking if we wanted to take the fan with us.

Men think they have it so bad when we are going through menopause. My husband reminds me that he is the one who has had to deal with my mood swings for what seems like the past 30 years. One night I had enough. I woke up at 2:30 in the morning with an ocean of water filling the multiple rolls between my top and my tummy. Ah yes, that lovely feeling is called night sweats; they can bring you out of the deepest sleep into believing the roof has leaked. I threw the sheets off and rolled toward my husband. The ensuing flood quickly drenched the sheets between us.

I got up, grabbed a robe and went out to the family room to sleep sitting up in the recliner with a fan pointed at me. I turned on the TV and tried to relax. About 15 minutes later my husband appeared...sheets in tow.

As he passed by me he said, "Baby, I am soooo sorry. Apparently I was sound asleep and didn't realize I had to go to the bathroom. I totally apologize!"

I know the right thing to say was, *"Oh no, Hun ... it was me and my night sweats."* But I looked at him and said, "Don't worry about it, Babe...it happens to the best of us."

What can I say here, girls? *Global warming* has a way of messing with our minds, our emotions, and our bodies. I knew the honest and right words to say, but I was really thinking, *Just Nuke Me Now*!

Just Debbie...

You can call it global warming, menopause, a hot flash, or whatever floats your boat, but I like to think of it as a "power surge". This sounds much better to me. The amount of steam we give off could run an entire fleet of ships, cars, houses, or anything else for that matter. If the world could be run by female power surges we would never need gasoline again. If you could bottle it, we could power the world. Can you imagine what we could do if we were able to channel all of our feminine heat waves for the good?

Every season of a woman's life is a lot like the "Wide World of Sports" with "The Thrill of Victory and the Agony of Defeat." In our case, it is more like "The Thrill of Romantic Fantasy" and "The Agony of Biological Reality". We started out as Cinderella waiting for our turn at the ball, but real life has been a little bit more like the "Survivor" reality series. They dropped us on an island and said, "Honey, here are a few supplies, and one primal man; good luck."

My favorite comedy show on TV has a certain mother-in-law who lives right across the street from her son. This out-law (I mean in-law) always has her hands in the kitchen, her nose in her daughter-in-law's business, and her apron tied right around you-know-who's neck. Did I mention that the father-in-law is sitting in the easy chair with his pants sadly unzipped? What's a girl to do? They call it comedy, but it is the familiar reality that makes us laugh out loud.

Not only do we have a pot-load of hormones to deal with, we must admit that our men are just different from us. There may be some truth in "Men are from Mars, Women are from Venus". Where we see tables filled with candles and gold chargers with beautiful seasonal place settings, our men see white paper plates and paper towels on TV trays in front of the big game. We see romance, cards, and flowers; they see a quick stop at the Circle K to take care of their holiday shopping. They think like men; we think like women. Will we resent our differences in the way we think and act or will they be drawn to the grace we offer?

Our lives are filled with seasons: fall, winter, spring, and summer. I love every season from planting spring flowers and enjoying their glorious colors, to cook-outs, watermelon, sparkling pools and campfire nights. After the heat of summer, I can't wait to decorate my house for fall and get ready for a day in the mountains and that first taste of hot apple pie. Even when it is still summer I am bargain shopping to find just the right Christmas presents for those I love.

One of my favorite traditions is cranking up the air-conditioning and turning on my fireplace for a "Christmas in July Party" complete with Christmas cookies. I actually enjoy wrapping Christmas presents in July. It makes me feel like I am ahead of the game...I just can't wait for Christmas to come. I love to savor every minute of the planning, the celebrating, the shopping, the singing, and everything else about that season.

This, my friend, is the thrill of fantasy, and who doesn't love to live there? I am a romantic at heart but I live in a real world, and that is not always easy for me.

We need to return to Proverbs 31 as it describes for us a godly woman who lived in the real world. What does this woman do with her emotions and her time? She has a "noble" character and is worth far more than a credit card can buy. "Noble"… now that's an interesting word. It means excellent, grand, and impressive. This woman ROCKED on her good *and* bad days … and I'm not talking about in a rocking chair.

Listen to the next part of Proverbs 31:12 NIV, *"She brings him [her husband] good, not harm, all the days of her life."* Verse 11 tells us that *"he trusts in her."* She is not competing; she is completing him. He knows she has their best interests at heart.

Her husband has confidence in her and she provides loving care for her family. She speaks with wisdom. She is a woman who fears the Lord and is to be praised. Before you get worn out just thinking of all she does, look at who she is trying to please and where she gets her strength. Also, notice that this woman does not do any of this out of guilt, exhaustion, or fear. She can actually laugh at the days to come, living without fear of the future because she has faith in the one who holds her future in His hands.

The Bible speaks of another woman who exemplifies nobility under great pressure. Her name was Esther. She became the queen in a time of great spiritual upheaval. Things were heating up all around her. God's chosen people, the Jews, were in great danger. Fearful, but still risking her own life, she decided to take a stand; one that could have cost her big time.

Esther's older cousin, Mordecai, spoke some powerful words to her at just the time she needed to hear them: *"Do not think that because you are in the king's house you alone of all the Jews will escape. For if you remain silent at this time, relief and deliverance for the Jews will arise from another place, but you and your father's family will perish. And who knows but that you have come to royal position for such a time as this?"* (Esther 4:13-16 NIV) Esther's response was this: *"I will go to the King, even though it is against the law, and if I perish I perish."*

She was willing to be the person God would use to expose the evil influence in the king's court; that influence could have ended her life and many others, as well. Esther offered herself willingly to be used by God to save her people.

Very simply, here is my theory on *global warming* for women. Every day we each face hot flashes from within and Esther-sized battles from without. Hot flashes are mandatory; power surges are optional. We get to choose how we handle the things that come our way. Our world is not getting better politically, spiritually, physically, morally, or otherwise.

If we wait for a perfect, cool, sunny day to take our stand, that day will never come. Each of these women was the *thermostat* in their homes and community, not the *thermometer*. They did not just reflect the rising temperatures around them; they changed the climate of their day for the better. With God's power flowing through them, there was a noticeable power surge.

So, the next time you feel global warming heating things up around you and the radiant heat is beginning to rise within you…when you feel like saying *"Just Nuke Me Now"*, remember that you are the *thermostat* not the *thermometer*. This is the autumn of your life … yes; your life is full of changes. Each of us has a question to answer in this life, Will we be changed by God's spiritual *power surge*? Perhaps it is to just start praying . . .

"God, I am ready to take my stand for You; so Just Nuke Me Now!"

Dancin' in the Rain

Funny Denise ...

        Have you ever met someone and felt in your heart of hearts something so familiar about that person that your soul felt at ease even before you know their name? That was Leslie.

        I met Leslie in the foyer of my church on a beautiful Sunday morning in 1993. I spotted her the minute I walked in and knew we were going to be great friends because she and I were the only two women still wearing "big hair" from the 80s. Leslie's personality radiated joy ... she was the type of person everyone wanted to be around.

        Leslie and I had some adventures together; one, in particular, was a trip we took to a women's retreat in the mountains. We laughed, talked, hiked and pretty much enjoyed everything God had to offer. One day as we were hiking our conversation turned to being flat-chested.

Leslie said, "I am just as flat-chested as you are."

I said, "LIAR!"

She said, "No, no … I have the answer for you."

I quipped, "If you are talking about the Wonder Bra, just save your breath. You have to have some sort of chest to see the wonder in that bra."

She said, "Now wait a minute … I got it at Victoria's Secret and it's a Water Bra."

I said, "A WHAT?"

She said, "Yep … it's a water bra. Come on … today we will go to the mall and get you a water bra. You will be amazed!"

So off we went to the mall to purchase my water bra. Leslie overcame my initial hesitation by telling me that you can put it in the freezer and wear it during the summer. I was all for that. We both live in the desert and anything COLD in the summer is well worth any money it costs.

We walked into Victoria's Secret and she went one way while I headed to the bras. She told me to feel each bra to see if it was water, gel, or padding. Do you know what kind of looks you get when you start fondling bras to determine if they are filled with gel or water?

In the midst of this awkward undertaking a sales clerk came up behind me and said, "Stretch out your arms so I can measure you for your bra."

I was thinking ... Whaaat???

She said, "Yes ... you should be a 34B."

Oh baby, I have found a miracle sales clerk if she thinks I am a 34B! Go ahead and measure me ... I am all for it!

Leslie walked up and, seeing me with my arms outstretched and the tape measure wrapped tightly around me, began to chuckle. The sales clerk handed me a great-looking water bra and sent me to try it on in the dressing room.

Now, here is the best part about Leslie. She would never leave your side when she knew you were struggling. So, I went into the dressing room and she sweetly stood outside giving play-by-play instructions on how to get the most out of - or should I say *into* - the water bra.

"Pull from the sides into the bra," she said. "Pull up from the stomach and pull all the loose skin into it ... this will work."

I said, "Well, I've got three double chins so I will just yank those in there too!"

To say I looked like I had been hit by the Enhancement Fairy would be an understatement, and I couldn't wait to get home to show my husband how absolutely fabulous I looked. I wore my new purchase out of the store and as we were laughing at our escapades through the mall Leslie said, "The best part about the water bra is that when you run ... you actually jiggle!" Not only did I jiggle that day but we giggled, too. It has been said, "A good friend is like a good bra ... they lift you up." Leslie was always uplifting.

My sweet friend, Leslie, was diagnosed with cancer and fought through treatment of that dreadful disease three times. She

54

had such a beautiful faith; the kind of faith that helped me grow too. It was amazing to be around her because she never gave up. She made it her mission to bring others to Christ while fighting this disease. I never saw her angry about what she was going through. She always wanted people to know that she faithfully believed God was doing what was best for her. If she could touch other people's lives through her struggle, then every step she took in her fight was worth it.

One day after she had started chemo, I called her and said, "I want to pick you up and take you to get your nails done. We can have lunch and just hang out." She was so excited. I owned a burnt orange jeep and decided the day was cool enough to take the top off so Leslie could get some fresh air. I picked her up and we started off for the mall about 10 minutes away. She was wearing a beautiful hat, and it was a good thing because the Santa Ana winds picked up as we were driving. I looked like Phyllis Diller on a bad hair day by the time we got there.

As we walked into the mall I said, "Well at least your hair is in place."

She smiled and said, "No, not really."

She removed her hat and I could see that the part in her hair was about three inches across, and more hair was falling out as we stood there. She laughed about it and said it was about time for her to shave it off but she wasn't sure how people would react to seeing her bald. She wasn't sure how she would react either.

I said, "Sweetie, listen up ... do you know how you can tell when somebody is drop-dead gorgeous? When they step out of a pool with wet hair and they are still beautiful ... that is YOU! Now, me, on the other hand ... I step out of the pool with wet hair and people think I am my brother ... big difference!"

Sunday morning came, and in she walked with a beautifully shaved head. I took off running to her with long arms and legs flailing everywhere (as Leslie would put it). I gave her a huge bear hug and told her how absolutely beautiful she was; and it was no lie. She actually was as beautiful without hair as she was with hair. She said that day was a turning point in her life fighting cancer. She had realized it wasn't about her; it was about saving others.

Throughout Leslie's battle with cancer she kept a blog. She wrote in that blog every day and chronicled her battle with that disease. But the blog wasn't just about her fight with cancer; it had many other parts. The first part was always something entertaining or uplifting. The second part was any news about her treatments. Next she would usually post a picture of somebody or something that touched her life the day before. She would list prayer requests for others and ask people to send in prayer requests so she could pray for them daily.

Leslie encouraged all of her readers to read the Bible in a year and would list the scripture verses for that day. She would end with the QOTD (Question of the Day) and these words ... "God is GOOD!" No matter what the news of her illness was ... whether good or bad ... Leslie always ended with "God is GOOD!"

Just Debbie . . .

Leslie never lost her faith; she never lost her encouraging words or her beauty, both inside and out. Her husband, children, and all of her friends would describe Leslie as "a little slice of Heaven" that constantly pointed us to God. We marveled to understand how Leslie could know that God was totally in control in spite of her long and painful suffering. How could she be filled with such joy and continue to remind us that God is good … all the time?

Have you ever asked Job-style questions? Why me? Why now? Why here? Where are you God? Don't you care? This kind of suffering is not a season that anyone would choose.

After loss, sometimes we begin to read God's Word from a different perspective. I wondered how Martha and Mary felt when they lost their brother Lazarus. The story of Lazarus is found in Luke 10 and it is a powerful read. Grab your Bible and let's take a look.

The first thing that jumps right off the page is that Mary is the one who poured expensive perfume on the Lord's feet and wiped them with her hair. We see that it was also Mary who sat at Jesus' feet to learn, while Martha worked in the kitchen and was busy with many things. Martha actually complained to Jesus about her sister, Mary. Jesus' response to Martha in Luke 10:42 was, *"There is only need of one thing"*. Mary had found what was most important, to worship God, and that would never be taken away from her. It was Mary who sat at Jesus' feet, and who "wasted" her expensive perfume, and then wiped those feet with her own hair.

When something bad happens, many of us are told it happened because we have sinned and are being punished. Yet, we see very clearly that Mary and Martha were not being punished by Jesus. They were just part of God's master plan.

I wonder if Mary wanted to question God, "Lord, I sat at your feet and I even poured out expensive perfume on your feet and this is the thanks I get? You are going to let my only brother die?" Sometimes we find that God's most faithful servants go through big trials.

We also see that the two sisters sent word to Jesus that their brother was very sick and asked Him to come. The message tells us something very important, *"Lord, the one you love is sick."* (John 11:3 NIV) Can you imagine not high-tailing it when your loved one is close to death?

If God is sovereign as the Bible says, then why does He not intervene to stop all suffering and keep our loved ones from pain and death? In this story, we see that Jesus knew, Jesus cared, and Jesus did not choose to stop it. Sometimes in life I am troubled by this thought, but I also know our view of pain is from a limited earthly perspective.

Finally, we see Jesus' response: *"Lazarus' sickness will not end in death. No, it happened for the glory of God so that God's Son may be glorified through it."* (John 11:4 NIV) The story goes on to tell us that Jesus stayed right where he was for two more days, until Lazarus died. Was God-in-the-Flesh punishing them, uncaring, or just late?

The scriptures tell us that the Jewish leaders were trying to devise a plot to kill Jesus. But Jesus was guided by a bigger plan, a different clock, and greater purposes than either Mary or Martha could understand. They had been chosen by God to be part of "The Glory Story".

Mary and Martha would each take their turn to meet Jesus when he finally came to town. After four days in the grave they both had the opportunity to meet Jesus face to face and say to Him, *"Lord, if you had been here, my brother would not have died."* The crowd then asked the question we all want to ask, *"This man healed a blind man. Why couldn't he keep Lazarus from dying?"* Why, WHY, **WHY**?

Jesus' response is simple. He goes to the tomb where Lazarus' decaying body lay and weeps. Can we begin to understand the response of God? He loves Mary, Martha, and Lazarus. He truly cares, and he comes. He is not punishing them for some sin.

He has not forgotten them, and he is deeply touched by their loss and grief.

Jesus' true calling is about to be revealed as He commands, *"Roll the stone away!"* (John 11:39) Finally, there comes a ray of light to all of us who cannot begin to understand what God-in-the-Flesh is here to teach us. Jesus says, *"Didn't I tell you that you will see God's glory if you believe?"* (John 11:40 NLT) On that day, Lazarus came back to life and God's glory was revealed.

Jesus is never late or surprised by our pain and suffering. As much as He loves us, and even weeps with us, He is guided by a higher eternal calling. We see today; He sees eternity. Earthly pain is not His greatest enemy; eternal pain through separation from God is.

When Jesus responds to Martha, he simply tells her, *"I am the resurrection and the life. Anyone who believes in me will live, even after dying. Everyone who lives in me and believes in me will never ever die. Do you believe this, Martha?"* (John 11:26 NLT)

This question is still the central question we need to answer in each of our lives today. When suffering comes, do we believe that Jesus is life? When death comes, do we believe that it is just the doorway to eternity? When God seems late, do we understand that His timing is always perfect? God is still sovereign in spite of sin and suffering.

Whenever Leslie blogged, she used the words: faith, hope, and love. She could describe God as "Good all the time" because she understood life in light of Heaven's perspective. She was on loan to us; she always belonged to her Heavenly Father.

Leslie was always writing encouraging notes to people and her influence and encouragement were felt far and wide. The timing of her notes could only have come from God, her heavenly father.

She repeatedly sent notes that would arrive at the exact moment suffering would strike.

Denise was going through medical tests and waiting for days for biopsy results that were being sent to multiple places. No one seemed to be able to decide if it was cancer. The morning she had to walk into the doctor's office, who do you think she got a card from? Not only did she receive a Cancer pin of Hope to wear, but do you think Leslie knew about it? Only Heaven's hotline works like that.

Denise mentioned that someone had told her they were sorry they had missed the drama in which she had acted the previous Easter which remembered Leslie's story. We agreed that we should put a chapter in our book to honor her. That day as we were having this little discussion, I was cleaning my home office and had eight jumbo bags of trash surrounding me. At the very moment I said we should include Leslie's story, I reached down to grab the next handful of papers and I picked up an empty envelope. The return address said Leslie Gilbert, and it was addressed to me. The hair on my neck stood up and I reached down to find the card that had been in the envelope. The card had a picture of two little girl angels on the cover.

On the inside of this long-forgotten card she had written me a note of encouragement. She told me how much she had loved a song that I had written at Christmas and encouraged me to continue writing. She ended her note by telling me how much she appreciated me, thanked God for me, and she signed it "with love".

You see, Leslie just had a way of breathing life into people. She is one of the reasons I am writing this book today. Her urgency and passion were truly contagious.

Leslie lived more in her 49 short years than most people could live in a thousand. It is truly not the amount of years in a life, but the amount of life in those years. We have no doubt that Leslie is living her life in Heaven just as she lived it on earth. She is loving God, loving life, and loving people. Her song goes on. We are just two of the people that have picked up the tune and are singing along with Leslie. What the scriptures tell us is so true; this is NOT all there is. Our life here is just a warm-up for the real Celebration.

I learned an important lesson from Leslie, "Because God is good all the time and He holds my future in His hands, I need to worry less and dance more. Nothing can separate me from God's love. So ... what is stopping me from living life to the fullest?"

And so I have begun living out the passion of my life ... writing. Thank you, Leslie, for the encouraging prompt. We all have but one life, one chance, and one amazing opportunity to shine for God. We dare not miss this dance.

I like to imagine Leslie Gilbert's arrival day in Heaven. I am sure Jesus said, "Welcome home, my good friend and faithful servant, Leslie."

I have a feeling that Jesus then turned to Heaven's great cloud of witnesses with a smile on His face and said . . .

"By Faith . . . Leslie Danced!"

61

Faithful through the Seasons:

Dedication to Leslie Gilbert

"WOOO HOOO! I am celebrating life today. This is my birth month, and I plan to celebrate every day, all month long as I enjoy all the amazing people that God has put in my life. God is good all the time . . . so I am *Happy Dancing*."

These were the kind of words that we looked forward to reading each and every day as we logged onto Leslie's blog to follow her Celebration of Life. Her fearless life lived in faith, joy, and hope has prompted us to dedicate this book to her. Leslie's blog, her smile, her life, and her love have left a mark on us for eternity. The amazing thing is that Leslie didn't live life in fear; instead, she was always "Livin' life LARGE

It is our desire to see death and life for what it really is, an opportunity to live life with faith overcoming fear. Our focus needs to be on the life God has given to each of us and our feet need to respond to the music of life with a dance.

"It's not the amount of years in a life; it's the amount of life in those years." It's the sort of thing we say when someone is taken from us too soon, but in Leslie's case it was so very true.

These words were the tribute that Leslie's husband, Mike, spoke about her at her Celebration of Life service. No one could say it better than Mike did...

"Leslie lived more in her 49 years than most people do in 100. Leslie loved to celebrate any occasion; she patented the 'birth-MONTH' celebration. She loved the holidays, especially Christmas. Every year from the beginning of October to the end of December, our house would be wall-to-wall decorations 'throwing up Christmas' she would say.

"The reason Leslie loved celebration was because Leslie loved people. Holidays are for family and EVERYONE was family to Leslie. Thanksgiving and Christmas Eve were times for family and the house was always full. She always invited some 'strays' too—people who didn't have any family near. Leslie always made everyone feel welcome. Serving others was one of her greatest joys. As hard as it is for me to say, cancer made Leslie a better person. It gave her a sense of urgency to encourage others, to foster relationships between people, and to share the love of God. Many of you read her blog every day and felt her radiant optimism. That optimism was real; it was not just putting on a brave face for the world to see.

"That is not to say that there were not hard times, but Leslie always held onto hope—she knew that God was in control and that He had a plan for her life. She said that her tribulations were all worth it if it brought people closer to God and to each other. Leslie never lost hope."

Perhaps you can now see why this dedication has to be bigger than just spoken words that tell you about Leslie. Leslie's faith was so alive that it was far reaching. With thanksgiving to God for her amazing life, we desire to use this book in a way that would honor her memory and continue to encourage women that are struggling, suffering, or just in need of some hope. By faith, we hope to give these books away to women in hospitals, cancer centers, and Leslie's beloved schools, to our community and beyond. Would you prayerfully join us in passing this message on to someone you know who needs encouragement right now?

Our dear friend, Leslie, was "faithful through the seasons" and this book has been given to you to share the secret that empowered her life. It is our prayer that together we can all follow in her footsteps ... and I can promise you that those feet are "Happy Dancing".

Epilogue: The Changing Seasons

"As long as the earth endures, seedtime and harvest, cold and heat, summer and winter, day and night will never cease."

—Genesis 8:22NIV

There are certain moments that we watch and wait for with great anticipation. The evenings are short, dark, and cold and everything seems dormant. Then one morning you awake to hear the birds singing and it smells like spring, and your heart skips a beat.

Before you know it, the days are getting longer and warmer. You just want to go sit out on a patio as the world is ablaze with color. The water is warm and inviting you to just jump in. Soon, the summer heat bears down on you…and about the time you are thinking you just can't take one more day of triple digit weather, you walk outside one evening and feel something different in the air. The west winds are blowing and fall is on its way. The days of brilliant color and changing leaves won't last very long, so, you take long walks and scenic drives to soak in this absolute beauty.

We chart our lives by these changing seasons. God's Word encourages us to pay close attention, *"Now learn this lesson from the fig tree: As soon as its twigs get tender and its leaves come out, you know that summer is near. Even so, when you see **all these things**, you know that the end is near, right at the door."* (Matthew 24: 32-33 NIV) What are "all these things"?

This passage goes on to tell us that these last days will be *"as the days of Noah"*. There was great wickedness on the earth back then, much like there is today.

There will be tribulation, false prophets, increased earthquakes, wickedness, and a lack of faith on the earth. Can we know when this interruption to the seasons will take place?

The disciples asked Jesus a very interesting question, "*Lord, are you at this time going to restore the kingdom to Israel?*" He said to them, "*It is not for you to know the times or dates the Father has set by His own authority.*" (Acts 1:6-8 NIV) He then tells them "*they would receive power from the Holy Spirit and they were to be witnesses for God to the ends of the earth.*"

We can all see that the "seasons are changing" for our world and not for the better. Yet, none of us knows the exact time God will choose to intervene in this fallen world or in our lives, personally. Noah and his entire family were saved through their faith in God: when He told them to build the boat and get in, they obeyed.

This book has really been about living a life of faith; we want to be able to "laugh at the days ahead." Perhaps we should just be honest and say right here that we find that dear Proverbs 31 woman intimidating to the MAX. We might as well just get that out there. She seems so perfect in all she thinks, says, and does. Where is the reality in her life? Doesn't she ever get tired? What would she be like if she was with us here and now?

That, my friends, is why we have shared with you Leslie's story. She faced all the struggles in this life with challenges beyond belief and yet she lived every moment of her life with strength, nobility, honor, and joy. She "laughed at the days ahead."

Perhaps you are wondering why in a book filled with grins and giggles we are telling you a story that involves a dear friend being in Heaven now. How can this message be of any comfort to anyone that is presently struggling with any kind of health issue? Is there a single one of us who can begin to fathom our mortality?

That is the proverbial elephant sitting smack-dab in the middle of our living room.

We don't want to hear any of this talk about Heaven, but we must all admit that we are secretly worried, fearful, and silent about this issue. I know what fear looks like. I have seen it close, up front, and personal. My husband, a friend and I survived a plane crash many years ago. The commercial jet we were on caught fire in the air, lost hydraulics, and came to a stop in a field after going off the runway, which caused the fuselage to break apart below our feet while the plane headed for an embankment. Yes, that was a day I will never forget! Nor, will I ever forget that I knew beyond a shadow of a doubt that the next face I would see would be that of Jesus, himself. We were miraculously saved; however, I have had a lot of dreams about planes since that time. I wish I could tell you that I am now fearless from that encounter but it just would not be honest on my part. I can tell you with complete certainty that was not our time.

My next encounter with life and death came with the birth of our daughter, Chelsea. I began seeing gold - my vision was breaking up; I was unable to sleep at night and was just feeling unexplainably weird. I went for my regular doctor's appointment and they could not get a fetal heart rate. Not only that, my blood pressure was dangerously high. They immediately hauled me to the hospital and I soon found myself having an emergency C-section before the epidural had time to kick in. They said there was no time to wait to save the baby or me. I found out within a few days that my premature baby girl had Down syndrome. This child has been a *gift of God* to us every single day of her life. God not only spared our lives, but He has since used all of this for His glory and our blessing. Once again, I had experienced the sovereign hand of God on my life.

In the last couple of years I have had some other encounters with the *great thief named fear*. Now fear is the opposite of faith, and it tries to come and steal our joy. It causes us to question and doubt, which puts us exactly where the enemy of God wants us to be.

My father recently had a stroke and has had Parkinson's which comes with a whole new set of issues including challenges with his memory. He has done amazingly well with all of these challenges but he requires constant care, so our family has had to move him into an assisted living home. This journey has not been easy or without pain, but God has provided and shown His loving care through all of it. I do not have the words to tell you all of the emotions that come with what I have described to you. All I can tell you is this; if I could give my dad anything, I would take a clock and turn back the hands of time so that he could live his life again, because it has been one amazing ride for God.

In the midst of these challenges and changes I have had some struggles of my own. On the very same weekend of my dad's stroke I had a tumor removed from my left cheek. It was pretty stressful at the time, but I am thankful it turned out okay. They discovered another tumor a short time later in my right arm. After having it removed, I was waiting on my pathology reports and a couple weeks went by; that is good news right? The night before I was to get the stitches out of my arm, I received a call from the receptionist saying, "The doctor wants to meet with you tomorrow morning first thing about your pathology report."

Shoot, that doesn't sound too good; and it wasn't. I know ... I know ... I lead an interesting life, but then again, maybe you do, too? I understand what it means to be fearful. To tell you the truth, I could write the handbook on fearful; I think we will call it "Chicken Dance"... but perhaps we should save that for next time. What we need to remember is that our God is Sovereign. He is sovereign over planes, children, health, lives, and all eternity. Satan, the enemy of God, cannot take us out without God saying, *"Yes, I have accomplished my perfect plan in your life, and now I am ready to welcome you home for your reward."* Worry will not add one single day to your life; it can, however, steal all your joy.

Today, if you are filled with whys, worries, and wonderings, we have a very important message to leave with you; God always provides the way out for each of us. Not one of us will live on planet earth forever, but we can live forever with God's gift of eternity.

Revelation 21:4 (NLT) tells us the rest of the story, *"He will wipe every tear from their eyes, and there will be no more death or sorrow or crying or pain. All these things are gone forever."*

We would be remiss to end this book without inviting you to receive Jesus into your heart and make a difference for God in this life. Today, my friend, if you are worrying about the length of your life, you can just hand that worry over to a God who lovingly holds your future in His hands. You have no worries if you have accepted the free gift of eternal life in Heaven given to those who accept Jesus as their personal Lord and Savior.

It is time for us to stop worrying and start living a contagious life of joy. When that day comes and we meet God face to face, there will be no more crying there, only laughing, and there will be no more grieving, only Happy Dancing. It will be a SWEET reunion when we see His face and hear His words,

"Would you like to dance?"

A Prayer for the Seasons

If you find yourself in a place of worry and fear right now, we invite you to join us in a prayer that will allow you to laugh at the days ahead and know you will never be alone.

God has a plan for your future. Will you stop and pray right now and allow Him to accomplish that plan in your life? If you do, you will be part of His amazing "Glory Story" because He specializes in using ordinary people for extraordinary purposes. I want my life to count, and I pray you do, too.

Will you stop and join me in this prayer right now?

Dear God,

I am small, but you are so big.

I feel stuck, but your power is unlimited.

I am filled with worry, but you bring peace.

I thank you for making a way for me today to walk out of the darkness and into the light.

Thank you, God, for delivering me from sin and death through your son, Jesus Christ.

I accept JESUS as my Lord and Savior; and acknowledge He is my God.

I am sorry for wasted days, wasted time, and wrong choices.

These have kept me from the dance that you have had in mind for me since the day you created me.

From this day on, I will hand you my worry,

And seek your plan, your peace, and your protection.

I pray all of this in Jesus' name.

Amen

It is time for a new season to begin in your life. So, get a Bible, find a great church that will be God's family to you, and find a really good friend to help you walk in faith versus fear. With God on your side, you will NEVER be alone...His Spirit will live in you.

Our Family Prayer

Last but certainly not least, we give thanks for our families. They have read our stories and encouraged us along the way, and for that we are very thankful. Our families are our greatest gifts. As we have written many of the stories in this book we are reminded that our most precious memories began as difficult times, but when seen in retrospect, they have become hilarious. Whether silly or serious, we recognize that "God is good" all the time.

The Proverbs 31 woman reminds us that a big part of being a woman of strength, nobility, and honor includes being the kind of woman who provides for the needs of her family. This kind of woman brought her husband "good all the days of his life." She received the living water from God versus finding the "sugary substitutes" that let us all down. It is our desire to be that kind of women. When our confidence and love come from God, alone, we will not be easily let down or disappointed if people do not fill all of our emotional needs, as no person can ever do. We can be free to love, live, and laugh because we know that God has covered us throughout the seasons of our lives.

Maybe you know God, but you are struggling in some important relationship in your life. We invite you to join us in one more prayer, *"God, make me the kind of woman of nobility, strength, and honor that you have called me to be. Help me not to seek changes in everyone around me, but instead, let me be changed. When the climate around me is less than ideal, let me be the "thermostat" that changes relational temperatures to reflect your glory. I know that I can never do this on my own, so just "Nuke Me Now" and before I walk out my door each and every day, let me put on my armor so I can "Spanx" the devil right out of my life.*

In Jesus strong and powerful name we pray! Amen.

Celebrating the Seasons Bible Studies:
Winter … A Time to Wait

"Praise be to the name of God for ever and ever; wisdom and power are his. He changes times and seasons. He deposes kings and raises up others. He gives wisdom to the wise and knowledge to the discerning."
--Daniel 2:20 -21(NIV)

Winter's Welcome: Describe a time in your life that was like "winter".

Winter Waiting's: Discussion (Romans 8: 18-27)

➢ What should we do when we are stuck in a time of silence, pain, and waiting?
➢ Why does God allow times of "winter storms" in our life?

Winter Wisdom: Lesson (Romans 8: 28-39) *(Fill in the blanks)*

➢ God works for the _____ of those that love Him and are called according to His purpose.
➢ God will be victorious over _____.
➢ God is "For us" and nothing can separate us from His _____.
➢ God's love is _____ in spite of evil.
➢ God's work is to make us "More than _____" in Him.

Winter's Work: Application-- Which of these are you struggling with? (James 1:1-21)

➢ Develops Perseverance (verses 2-3)
➢ Makes us complete and mature (verse 4)
➢ Causes us to ask God for wisdom (verse 5)
➢ Helps us to learn to trust God without doubting (verse 6-8)
➢ Brings us a reward from God (verse 13)
➢ Brings about God's righteousness (verse 21)
➢ Helps us to humbly accept the word planted in us (verse 21)

"Let us not become weary in doing good, for at the proper time we will reap a harvest if we do not give up." —Galatians 6: 9(NIV)

Spring . . . A Time to Plant

"Those who plant in tears will harvest with shouts of joy.
They weep as they go to plant their seed,
but they sing as they return with the harvest."--Psalm 126:5-6 (NLT)

Spring Brings: Icebreaker

> ➤ Why does spring make us feel alive and refreshed?
> ➤ After you have gone through a time of dormancy and winter winds, have you seen God bring something new "to you" or "through you"?

Spring's Seeds: Discussion—the Spiritual battle for our soul
(Matthew 13:3-23)

> ➤ This passage contains three parables that teach us about planting. The parable of the sower tells us about the spiritual battle that happens in this life with regard to the Word of God. Who are the farmer, the field, and the enemy?
> ➤ The Parable of the weeds focuses on the harvest. Who is in charge of the harvest?
> ➤ The Parables of the mustard seed and the yeast help us understand the power of a small seed and of yeast that is added to bread. What needs to happen for the seed to be strong and grow?

"Spanx the Devil": Lesson-- Fill in the blanks (Eph. 6:10-18)

> ➤ The armor of God in this passage means we are to put on the mighty power of God and walk in God's _____.
> ➤ Much like military armor, the full armor of _____ includes these pieces: belt of truth, breastplate of righteousness, boots of peace, shield of faith, helmet of salvation, and the sword of the Spirit.

Spring Forth: Application (Psalm 126:5-6)

> ➤ How is pain and planting related?

Summer . . . A Time to Climb

"A wise youth harvests in the summer, but one who sleeps during harvest is a disgrace."—Proverbs 10:5(NLT)

My Top 5 Exercises: Jumping to conclusions, Flying off the handle, Carrying things too far, Dodging Responsibilities, Pushing my luck

Summer Stretch: Icebreaker

> ➤ How do you feel about exercise?
> ➤ What kind of exercise best suits you and why?

Summer Sapped: Discussion (Psalm 32:1-7)

> ➤ Why was David's strength being sapped from him like the summer heat? (Psalm 32: 4)
> ➤ Psalm 32 lays out for us the steps to freedom when we find ourselves in this situation. What steps did David take and what did he find out about God?

Summer Steps (Hebrews 12:1-11) **The training of discipline:**

1) Throw off everything that hinders us.
2) Stay away from sin that entangles us.
3) Run the race with perseverance.
4) Fix our eyes on Jesus.
5) Consider what Jesus did for us.
6) Don't grow weary or lose heart.
7) Remember that God disciplines those He loves.
8) As a child loved by God, endure hardship as discipline.
9) Submit to the Father and live.
10) Later on you will receive a harvest of righteousness and peace.

Summer Strong: Application (2 Corinthians 12:10)

> ➤ How do you feel about being weak? How can we be strong in our weakness?

Harvest ... A Time to Reap

"No discipline seems pleasant at the time, but painful. Later on, however, it produces a harvest of righteousness and peace for those who have been trained by it."—Hebrews 12:11(NIV)

Harvest Praise: What blessings are you most thankful for?

Harvest Prayers: Discussion (Matthew 9:37-38)

> ➢ There is a great need for servants. In prayer we can best know where God is leading us to serve. Where is He guiding you?

Harvest Preparation: Three Parables of the Harvest
(Matthew 25:1-45) (Fill in the blanks)

> ➢ **Time—The Ten Virgins** (Matthew 25:1-13)
> Only _____ of the virgins took the time to prepare for the Bridegroom's return. The warning is this, "Keep watch, because you do not know the day or hour."

> ➢ **Talents—Parable of the Talents** (Matthew 25:14-30)
> Two servants managed their master's talents and doubled what they were entrusted to watch over. One servant was called wicked and lazy as he _____ his. What he was given was taken away and given to someone else.

> ➢ **Treasures—The Sheep and the Goats**
> (Matthew 25:31-45)
> When we feed the poor or sick, visit someone in prison, or clothe someone in need, Jesus says that we have done this unto
> _____.

Harvest Participation: Application (Matthew 25:29)
> ➢ What gift of time, talent, or treasure has God given you that you could use for Him and how can you begin to meet practical needs?

The Barefoot Authors

The barefoot authors, Debbie Sempsrott and Denise Rogers, are excited to present three new books in 2013/2014: "Happy Dance", "Tubular Therapy" and "Our Faith Floats".

Each book cover shows feet without shoes. In Exodus 3:5b, Moses encountered Almighty God and was simply told *"Take off your sandals, for the place where you are standing is holy ground"* (NIV). These images remind us that the same God still speaks, rescues, and provides today. We call ourselves the barefoot authors because *our shoes are off, and we stand in awe of a God that takes the ordinary and turns it into 'Holy Ground'*.

Debbie Sempsrott is a preacher's kid, pastor's wife, and the mother of two. As a mother she has joined the "sisterhood" of special needs, and of adoptive moms. She serves in the area of worship and women's ministries. She is a graduate of Lincoln Christian College (Lincoln, Illinois) and Pacific Christian College (Fullerton, California) with BA's in music and education. She also holds a Master's Degree in Marriage and Family Counseling from Hope

International University (Fullerton, California). Most of all she is best known as "Just Debbie". She is the girl next door that loves to play, laugh, and swim in any nearby pool. She is the Ethel who is writing with her best friend, Lucy. She will break the mold on stereotypes for pastors' wives and put the "awe" in each and every story.

Denise Rogers is a graduate of McMurry College (Abilene, Texas). She is an accountant who co-owns her own bookkeeping business. Numbers roll through her mind from morning to night. However, she is not like any accountant you have ever met. She is as funny as the day is long. She has the red hair, antics, and facial expressions of Lucy; and yes, most everyone loves her! Denise is the wife of a "red-neck", mother of a firefighter, a church treasurer, and the person that is called on to speak when they need things to be funny ... really funny. That is the only way "she rolls". She is the queen of Spanx and the one that we call "Funny Denise". After you read a bit, I think you will agree this girl is pure "CWAZEE". She dares to say out-loud what the rest of us only think.

The Barefoot authors' message is one of honesty, hilarity, and hope. Each book contains grins and giggles, tears and triumphs, and hope and healing for the seasons of a woman's soul. You will laugh ... you will cry ... you will laugh until you cry. Your cares will grow smaller, and your view of God will grow larger. When you lay each book down you will simply stand in awe of a God who meets each one of us privately, personally, and providentially. The God of Moses is still alive, real, and intervening in our daily lives. He cares. He comforts. He comes near.

Together our shoes will come off, and we will stand in awe of a God that takes the ordinary and turns it into *'Holy Ground'.*

Denise and Debbie are available to speak for women's events and retreats. You can contact us at <u>www.ourfaithfloats.com</u>.

More Book Fun Awaits:

"Tubular Therapy: Facing Fear with Friendship & Faith"

Tubular Therapy is the story of one answered prayer, an unlikely friendship, and the God who meets us in the "rapids of life". This story of friendship and faith is one crazy ride down life's lazy river. It's a grand adventure with ups and downs, hilarity and heartbreak, that will make you shake your head in disbelief.

This Lucy and Ethel will take you on adventures like the Vichy shower, massages with Greta the Glute Meister, a bathroom slide down a mountain hill, and a near miss on a mountain road with an angelic encounter. We dare to talk about what most keep hidden deep inside. We'll float a while and talk awhile …We'll laugh a while and cry a while …Together we will experience God's healing touch and go home better than when we came!

"Tubular Therapy"
Is LOL healing for the woman's soul!

"Our Faith Floats"—Hope, Hilarity, and Healing for Women

From infertility, adoption, special needs, to the terrible twos and beyond, this book will make you laugh and make you cry; From the "turbo toilet" to baggage claim we hope you will chuckle.

This is the cruise of our lives. We are here to celebrate!! If it rains, we will get out and dance in it … If there are high winds we will grab a hand and hold on for dear life. Our cruise has a limited time-frame; every moment is precious. Choosing the cruise is simply choosing to love, live, and laugh because even when the high winds come we know that the God of the universe is right there in our boat. He stills the storms then and now … So, all aboard we dare not miss the cruise …

When you are done laughing and crying with us, we hope you will agree that "Our Faith Floats"!

High Stress … High Seas …High Hopes
… Never forget who's in your boat!

Join the Dance!!!

"There is a time for everything, and a season for every activity under Heaven ...

A time to be born and a time to die ...

A time to weep and a time to laugh ...

A time to mourn and a time to DANCE."

--Ecclesiastes 3: 1-4 (NIV)

Now is our time and we invite you to join us in the dance! We want to reach women that are weeping and help them laugh again. These books have been given away free of charge to: Hospice, a women's prison, hospitals, cancer centers, Chemo Angels, and to a Ronald McDonald House ... and the dance goes on!

If you would like to give these books away in your area please contact us and we can partner with you for a minimal price of about $2.00 per book, plus shipping.

Also, Denise and Debbie are available to come and speak for retreats and other events for women. We would love to bring "Happy Dance" books with us for your women, and to share with you the message of "Happy Dance".

We invite you to blog with us at www.ourfaithfloats.com.

Also, you can friend us at "Our Faith Floats" on Facebook.

You can also reach Debbie at **dsempsrott@roadrunner.com.**

Wishing you "Fabulous through the Seasons"